Normand Jones

BRIDGE TO SUCCESS

Getting from where you are in life to where you want to be!

"In light of knowledge attained, the happy achievement seems almost a matter of course, and any intelligent student can grasp it without too much trouble. But the years of anxious searching in the dark, with their intense longing, their alterations of confidence and exhaustion and the final emergence into the light -- only those who have experienced it can understand it."

Albert Einstein.

Copyright © 2009 Normand Jones
Original title: Bridge to Success
Original publisher: Jones Mediation & Coaching

Contributors:
Editing: Sandra X. Jones
Cover design: Estelle C. Timmerman

ISBN – 978-90-814937-1-0
NUR – 450/728/807

Any part of this book may only be reproduced, stored in a retrievable system and/or transmitted in any form, by print, photo print, microfilm, recording, or any other means, chemical, electronic or mechanical, with the written permission of the publisher.

This book is dedicated to:

My father John A. Jones

Whose persistence and determination led him to find the most beautiful and intelligent woman in the world to share his life. I am grateful for the combination of attitudes and characters that both were vital in the manifestation of the person I now am.

And:

My mother Gertrude C. Cham
Whose love and never ending care was the inspiration that led me to understand the value of attention and care. In fact; without the care I received from my mother I would have not been able to write bridge to success.

Introduction..9

1 Create your Idea 12

  1.1 Imagine your future to create it..................12

    1.1.1 The Power of imagination...................14

    Function of your belief system. 15

    1.1.2 Conflicting elements between Imagination and knowledge.......................21

    1.1.3 The power of knowledge....................24

    1.1.4 Unification of imagination and knowledge. 28

    1.1.5 The power of believing; everything is possible. 32

    1.1.6 How to imagine 35

  1.2 Decide to do what is needed to grow your thoughts into reality...39

    1.2.1 Idea in action..43

  1.3 Allow your expectations to exceed your imaginative potential. 47

    1.3.1 Bridge to physical manifestation of your idea. 48

    1.3.2 In control of expectations. 51

    1.3.3 Expectations; detours from life's highway. 52

    1.3.4 First step into the unknown.................53

1.3.5 How to neutralize deflection. 56

1.3.6 Why do we remain within our comfort zone?................59

1.3.7 Writing on the wall................62

1.3.8 Where do expectations come from....66

1.3.9 Poor little Nick. 67

1.4 Analyze your point of origin in relation to your destination................71

1.4.1 Where are you now? 72

1.4.2 Different perspectives. 74

1.4.3 Outside the comfort zone. 76

1.4.4 What is wrong with the comfort zone? 78

1.4.5 The professional approach. 79

1.4.6 Learn by example. 84

1.4.7 CARE in a nutshell, part one. 86

2 Apply................90

2.1 Learn by example, take the positive approach. 90

2.1.1 The lessons learned. 93

2.1.2 Message from the universe. 95

2.1.3 To be conscious of the teachers words. 98

2.1.4 The EGO has landed. 100

2.1.5 Misperception of the EGO.................102

2.1.6 Back and forth..104

2.2 Take initiative, control is your responsibility...107

2.2.1 Conviction makes taking initiative easy...112

2.3 Verify that every step you take brings you closer to your goal..116

2.3.1 Living in the moment........................118

2.3.2 Why are we blind to the moment?..120

2.3.3 Benefits of our limitations................122

2.4 Use the energy you create as your compass..126

2.4.1 Energy versus time............................127

2.4.2 Building bridges................................134

2.4.3 CARE in a nutshell; part two............137

3 Reflect...142

3.1 Examine the effect of your idea................142

3.2 X-Factor, gifts we receive but cannot unwrap..146

3.2.1 My father's prison walls...................147

3.2.2 How my father's prison walls became mine...151

3.3 People..154

3.3.1 The art of giving and receiving........155

3.4 Love = E=MC² = Consciousness...........158

   3.4.1 The source of the writings on our walls....................158

      Judaism....................159

      Christianity....................160

      Islam and Arab religions....................163

      Eastern religions Buddhism....................164

      Hinduism....................165

   3.4.2 How to vibrate love....................166

   3.5 Overcome ideas that hold you captive where you are....................171

   3.6 Revisit the creative process....................174

   3.7 Enhance your idea....................176

4 Energy....................179

   4.1 Behave according to your core values...179

      4.1.1 Belief, the driving force behind behavior....................179

   4.2 Express your true identity....................185

   4.3 Make your intentions clear on every level....................190

      4.3.1 Circumstances....................191

      4.3.2 Critical mass....................193

4.3.3 Who are you and your intentions?..196

4.3.4 Who is driving your car?...................200

4.4 Go for win-win through negotiations....204

4.4.1 Obstacles in communication.............206

4.4.2 Effective use of communication 212

4.5 Be genuinely you. 216

4.5.1 What is at the centre of your heart? 219

5 Epilogue. 222

Introduction

Yes, this is it!

You know and I know that, the fact that you have this book in your hands means that you have questions for which you believe the answers could be found in this book.

The title probably caused you to assume that by reading *Bridge to success* you will find answers to your questions about living a successful life.

Well, let me warn you right now.

In one way or another you will find answers to your questions. However, be advised that these answers can only help you 80% of the way, the other 20% will be your responsibility!

Here you will find exactly what is needed to build a bridge between where you are now in life and where you want to be.

I will show you how to build the bridge and how to cross it with the right tools.

This is not a book about construction, philosophy, history or spirituality. It's a practical guide to help you be conscious of your role in the midst of all that lives. And, it will show you how to assume the responsibility that goes with that role.

Bridge to success is a book about creating the life you choose to have and living it. I've done this, and now the feeling of absolute confidence and knowing that whatever tomorrow brings will be needed and accepted with open arms, prompted me to search for answers to why I am always so fortunate to consistently and continually have everything I need.

After more than 20 years of building a successful career in finance I decided to start following my heart more than my head. Now seven years later my beautiful wife, Mirjam with whom I've been together for about 20 years, and I, enjoy the blessing of three healthy and beautiful children, Kiran (8), Sarah (6) and Louise (3).

Since my career change I set up a successful practice for mediation and coaching, which enabled me, most of the time to work from home. At the same time I gained full control over my schedule and thus could plan my work around the family life. Now I am in the situation where I am, on all levels, living my dreams.

I remember as a child often talking about helping at least 5 million people before I die. This thought I've kept with me my whole life, and along the way I've arranged my private life in the service of others. I've managed to convert my hobby into my profession and now I am, as a mediator and personal/life coach, also helping others.

Ask yourself: what is the first thing that you needed directly after your very first gasp for breath on the day you're born?

And, as time passed, did the way care was given and needed not change?

Whichever way you look at it, CARE, in any form and at any time, is vital to whatever captures your attention and you wanting to become a success.

Think about projects you did at school or at work, your first love, having children, pets or anything you ever embarked upon, and you will see, without the proper care, you will at some level lose the connection that would otherwise bring you success.

I have managed to analyze the different components of CARE and created the CARE system which will be further discussed in details in Bridge to Success.

Once you apply the **CARE** system properly then the only logical consequence will be **YOUR SUCCESS!**

1 Create your Idea

Intention is the active partner of attention; it is the way we convert our automatic processes into conscious ones.

-Deepak Chopra-

1.1 Imagine your future to create it.

Take a moment, look around you. It doesn't matter where you are, in a room or outside in the park. What do you see? Now close your eyes and create a picture in your mind of 5 things, living or objects, which you've seen. Can you do this?

Don't worry; there is nothing wrong with you if you could not create the pictures.

There are still two other ways through which people use their imagination. Besides picturing things (visual), some people imagine through sound (auditory) and others through feeling (kinesthetic). Use the way that suites you best to imagine what you've observed.

Was it possible for you to imagine the things you've seen?

Now choose one and try **not** to imagine it. Try again...

Hmm you can't not imagine or visualize something you have just seen or observed, right?

Ok, let's try something else.

Let's take your house, car, bicycle or your watch. Do you remember the first time ever having these things? What went through your mind at that moment? Was it something like yes, this is it. I've reached my goal?

Do you know that every goal you ever had and still do has gone and is going through the same creative process?

Did you also know that the first step in this process is to imagine?

You first imagine using your heart, mind and body to tap into your spiritual or higher self, and then decide to do what is needed to bring your idea to life, find out if what you expect of it is indeed what you want it to be. Then you analyze where you are in the process of getting it and determine the distance you still need to travel to get you what you've imagined. To create anything you need to take these four basic steps, which I will discuss extensively further on. I'm not asking you to believe me at face value. However, I am asking you to believe in YOU!

Take yourself back to that moment at the notary when you received the key to your home, the first time you stepped into the car you just bought, the first bicycle ride on your new bike or putting your new watch on for the first time. Then go back somewhat further in time, to the first moment when you we're thinking about having any one of these items. From that moment press on 'play in slow motion' and allow your thoughts to revisit every step of the process and I am sure you will come up with these simple four steps I now call IDEA, which stands for Imagine - Decide - Expect and Analyze.

1.1.1 The Power of imagination

To create is only the first step in the CARE system that I will present to you further on in *Bridge to success*. When you apply the CARE system you will achieve success in all fields of life. Your professional career, family life and personal life will all, without limitations, join together and taste the success that comes with CARE.

You will find the balance to bring you long term and consistent success in all parts of your life at the same time.

In the previous chapter I introduced the concept of IDEA, which is the foundation on which everything is created. The three first components of CARE; Create, Apply and Reflect are the active part CAR. When you take charge, put yourself in the driver seat and drive this car using all of the tools at hand. You will create the energy flow that will carry you where ever you want to go. The energy that you create will represent who you are.

CARE is focused on finding out where you are in life, knowing where you want to be, getting you there and ultimately knowing and being you on all levels.

For now I want to pick up where I left off and talk some more about the enormous power of imagination.

Remember earlier you couldn't, **not** imagine something that you had already imagined?

Why is this? The answer is that your belief system won't allow you to.

Function of your belief system.

Before I continue, I will take a side step to explain the function of your belief system. In today's world belief systems are considered to be religions, ideologies, philosophies, worldviews, or ways of life. A belief system always has an ideology or philosophy; it is a collection of ideas and serves as a framework for organizing thought and action. Belief systems explain where the world comes from and where it's going; what our purpose in it is; how society should be organized; how people should treat each other; what to do when you make a mistake. Our beliefs bring us comfort and allow us to channel our energy.

When put in a broader perspective a belief system in general provides support for the social system. But even though it acts as a point of reference to support and justify our behavior, belief systems have a built-in purging mechanism which makes it flexible.

Now that we are clear on what belief systems and their functions are, I will continue to explain what I mean by who you are will not allow you to erase what you know.

Because you consciously looked at, and visualized that object you allowed it to become a part of you. And to erase it would mean erasing a part of you. It is the same as cutting off your leg.

My sister, Altagracia once told me a story about a lady who lived in a nursing home where she worked. Joyce, as the elderly lady was called couldn't walk and it was difficult for her to bend down and reach her feet. Often she called the nurses to help her scratch her feet, as she suffers from itching. When the nurse came and scratched her right foot she would say: 'not that one the other one.' This was confusing for the nurse as Joyce only had one leg. However, in her mind there was no doubt about the fact that her left foot was itching. This symptom is called Phantom pain. And it is the same effect that you will have should you, for whatever miraculous reason, succeed in erasing any information that is registered in your system.

What you've seen; car, dog, table, fruit basket etc. was raw information, until you became conscious of it. Then the function of your short-term and long-term memory kicked in and added value to it. In your short- term memory interpretation and decoding took place while in your long-term memory social and cultural values were added. Then again, the information was decoded, but this time based on your values as part of your social and cultural surroundings. It looks like a long process when reading about it, but all of this happens in a split second. Every day, hour, minute, second or part of a second this process is taking place thus forming your identity from your perspective and the perspective of everyone you are in contact with.

As a result an invisible web is spanned that encapsulates how you see yourself, the object, a person or group of people in your memory and your experiences. This web is packaged in your mind and sealed with a special code to unlock the information in the same sequence in which it was packaged. Now all it takes is that code, which can be a scent, sound, word or any other trigger to make the link visible and instantly you will reproduce your image of that object and the feeling that goes with it.

You might argue that information can be forgotten. Yes, but that's not the same as erasing it. Due to illness your belief system, on a conscious level, may be confused by the signals you unconsciously send out when the code is used.

However, what happens as a result of a long time passing is that the image you once produced will not have been erased but adapted according to your new belief system.

This is why, as a child you can picture your grandparents home to be huge, with an enormous yard and fence three times your size, and this picture remains with you as you grow up, only to find out after 20 years when you return, that the house is not bigger than the average home with a small yard and the fence is half your size.

Because your belief system is used to provide information to your imagination, you might say that your imagination is dependent on what you believe. This is not true: however, we often allow our beliefs to disrupt our imagination or sometimes even to hold it hostage, due to the values we add to the raw information.

I will tell you more about this later, but now I want to make a point. Please allow me to take you through the process again.

Imagine a famous building like the Sydney Opera House in Australia, the Eifel Tower in Paris, the Casa Mila in Barcelona, the White House in Washington DC, Buckingham Palace in London, the Royal Palace at the Dam in Amsterdam or any other famous building you can think of. Today you can imagine this building because it has become part of you. Just like your grandparent's home you can reproduce whatever this building means to you instantly via an emotion, picture or sound in your mind. This can be triggered by a word, scent, sound, person, and group of people or reading about it in this book.

Now ask yourself, would you be able to imagine this building if it never had existed? No? Well someone did a long time ago. That is why it is standing where it is today.

And isn't it funny that after all these years you could be standing in a picture that was once created in the minds of people like Jørn Utzon, Maurice Koechlin and Emile Nouguier, Antoni Gaudi, James Hoban, John Nash and Edward Blore, Jacob van Campen or any other architect you might think of.

Yep, all of these famous architects went through the same steps! In our minds these buildings represent who these people are. However, that is something only these famous people can decide about. I say this because the steps were taken in a process aimed at achieving success in one specific field of their lives. The CARE system is designed to bring you success in **every** field of your life.

By understanding the power of IMAGINATION you've taken the first step in the process of creation. But before I go on to show you how to imagine effectively there are some obstacles that need to be dealt with.

1.1.2 Conflicting elements between Imagination and knowledge.

In most societies a majority of people believe that knowledge is the most important thing to have. As a result of the overwhelming belief in this idea, social, cultural, political, legal, religious and other systems are structured in such a way that people presumed to have knowledge take the lead.

Since Albert Einstein expressed his thoughts with the words *"Imagination is more important than knowledge"*, there is an ongoing debate between people who believe this to be true and others who believe knowledge to be more important.

As time, for me, is limited to the duration of me being alive, I actually find it irrelevant which is more important as I am only interested in the question; How can I combine the power of both and apply them in my life to make me successful?

To answer this question I will explain the power of knowledge in this section. You can then decide for yourself if indeed imagination is more important than knowledge and how relevant this is to you.

Bridge to success is about giving you tools to build your bridge between where you are now and where you want to be, offering you instructions on how to use these tools effectively and reaching out to help you cross the bridge when you are ready.

Just like imagination, knowledge is a great tool to use when going for success. But before you can use it effectively you must know what it is and how it works.

Knowledge can simply be defined as knowing, through study, experience or tradition. The Oxford English Dictionary defines knowledge as 1 (a) Awareness or familiarity gained by experience (of a person, fact or thing) (b) A person's range of information. 2 (a). A theoretical or practical understanding of a subject, language etc, (b) The sum of what is known. 3. Philos, True, justified belief; certain understanding, as opposed to opinion. 4= Carnal knowledge. Come to one's knowledge become known to one. To my knowledge (i) So far as I know, (ii) As I know for certain.

And so, there are additional definations through different sources like:

(i) expertise, and skills acquired by a person through experience or education; the theoretical or practical understanding of a subject, (ii) what is known in a particular field or in total; facts and information or (iii) awareness or familiarity gained by experience of a fact or situation. The term knowledge is also used to mean the confident understanding of a subject with the ability to use it for a specific purpose if appropriate.

But, after having read these definitions can you truly tell me what knowledge is?

I don't think so!

Even some of the most learned scholars amongst us today are still engaged in philosophical debates which in general started with Plato's view on knowledge as "**Justified true belief**". Today there is still no single agreed definition of knowledge and no prospect for one, as there remain numerous competing theories.

However, there is some kind of consensus on the fact that the acquisition of knowledge involves complex cognitive processes: perception, learning, communication, association and reasoning. OK, what does this all mean?

For me it means that like imagination, knowledge goes through a similar process of information being interpreted and decoded in your short-term memory while in your long-term memory social and cultural values are added. Then again, the information is decoded but this time based on your values as part of your social and cultural surroundings. The difference between the two is where the information originated and whether or not it was pre-defined.

1.1.3 The power of knowledge.

Imagination comes through your mind by use of raw information or own interpretation of predefined information. Knowledge comes from researched information of the manifestation of what you have imagined. In other words; with imagination you can tap directly into the source of the unknown, the field of all possibilities and thus open doors to invite even the things that perceivably do not exist to become known. While knowledge, through science explores the right of existence of all that is known. This is how knowledge offers some sense of security, something tangible to hold on to. However, I sincerely believe that, unless the end of time presents itself to us, we cannot know anything for sure. And therefore we use knowledge to give us that sense of security.

If I ask you; is the world round? Or is your heart in the left side of your chest?

Without a blink of an eye, your answers will most probably be: yes, and again definitely yes!

These are things you are convinced to be true, because you know.

But just like you today believe the world is round, hundreds of years ago people believed the earth was flat and that the heart was in the head.

The point is not how long ago people believed the world was flat but the fact that in school we were taught that people for a long time lived their lives according to this belief. And because this knowledge was given to us through learning it became something that we know.

Now let me ask you a third question. But before I ask the actual question I would like to check with you if the feeling of life and happiness or heat and light would be a fair assessment of what the sun means to you. Take a moment to understand what I mean. To you, the sun is light and heat and you feel life's energy flowing through your body making you feel happy when you think of the sun and enjoy vacation time in the sun?

If your answer is yes, then please answer the following question; can you physically touch the sun? No? This is the answer I hoped for. If your answer is yes, then I congratulate you. But if your answer is no, then I will show you how you touch the sun! But before I do, I want you to not allow yourself to be confused by thinking this is a mind game. It is pure logic.

Now, imagine a sunny day on the beach. Surrounded by crystal white sand you're laying on your easy chair gazing towards the sea as the heat soaks into the tissues of your skin. At this point would you consider that the sun is touching you?

Ok, you choose to hesitate. I will change the question. Is heat touching you, the same heat we agreed was the sun?

Ok, I know it's hard to replace old things with new things. However, I believe that we have established that the sun is touching you. And now comes the scary part.

Do you know why it's scary? I will tell you. At this moment your belief system is considering itself under attack and has no other option than to fight back. One of the most powerful instructions engraved in the DNA of anything that lives is to survive. And as your belief system is alive it will fight to survive.

That is why in the first instance you hesitated and in a while you will forget to breathe. Saying this doesn't make me a Psychic. It is pure logic that while the sun or anything else is touching you, you are also touching the sun or that object. Are you convinced that you can physically touch the sun? If not, then ask the person closest to you to touch you. Then ask yourself are you touching this person too? Don't make it more difficult than it is; the person should be touching you, not your clothes. How does that feel? Do you now **believe** that you are touching this person?

This in fact brings us to my view; the closest any human can get to knowing is through belief. I will tell you exactly what I mean.

Earlier I mentioned that our belief system disrupts and sometimes holds our imagination hostage. Well, in addition to your struggle with the idea of your ability to touch the sun, this is what happens; because we so blindly believe in the almighty power of knowledge everything that does not correspond with what we know is a threat to us and will therefore be actively and ruthlessly surpressed.

This doesn't mean in any way that knowledge is superior to imagination or vice versa. But what it means is that we choose to believe as if we know, because of the sense of security that comes with knowledge. Any time we are challenged to let go of what we believe to know, we experience this as letting go of the sense of security we enjoy holding on to. Some call this 'comfort zone'.

Are you familiar with how it feels when you are afraid? Could you describe what happens to you? Is it like your heart begins to pound faster, dizziness, chest pains or overall losing control over your muscles? Even if you have these symptoms in the slightest form it means that you are experiencing an anxiety attack to some degree. Should you feel the need to become angry or even physical, then that's the sign that you believe that escape is close to impossible. And fighting is your only option to keep you in your comfort zone. In simple terms; knowledge puts you in your comfort zone and it is your duty to defend and protect. This means that whenever your imagination takes you outside of your comfort zone you will experience some kind of resistance and sometimes even a heavy internal battle taking place to get you back inside.

1.1.4 Unification of imagination and knowledge.

Having explained about the ongoing conflict between imagination and knowledge, I feel the urge to make a bold statement, so here it goes. I dare to imagine that in Albert Einstein's explanation of the formula $E=MC2$, where he stated that mass and energy are both but different manifestations of the same thing, is based on the principles that I use to say the same of Imagination and knowledge.

I truly believe that it is intention that lies at the core of knowledge and everything that can be imagined. The different manifestations of intentions into imagination or knowledge are due to slight differences in interpretations.

Now you must accept that the trick is to understand that both imagination and knowledge are important and they are both part of you. Instead of allowing them to fight for leadership you must find a way to combine and make use of both in favor of your life achievements. While I think about this, my thoughts take me back to one hot summer day while on vacation in Malta. Taking a walk through the streets of Valeta I walked into a small souvenirs shop. While looking through a stack of plasticized sheets of paper my attention was captured by one of the scriptures that sounded something like this;

"The situation was tense the call for a new leader was dominant. All leaves where revoked and everyone was summoned to attend a late night meeting, during which a new leader was to be choosen. After a few hours of discussion the legs teamed up and argued that it is more than fair that they become the leaders as they take the body

wherever it need to go and that is what a good leader does. The brain protested stating that without instructions from the brain the legs would be useless and besides, a good leader must have a helicopter view and decide on important matters. Well, well, well, said the hart if this is the case then I am the most important organ in the body. I am in charge of the distribution of blood, this is the most important job, and if I do not send any blood to the brain then the brain cannot function. Everyone was exhausted as the meeting went on endlessly. As noon the following day was approaching a timid voice, for the first time heard during the whole session spoke out saying; Excuse me, I know I'm not the brightest in the room and I know the work I do isn't as important as any of yours, however, as you cannot seem to come to a decision why can't I be the boss? An instant silence filled the room. For a few seconds you could hear a needle drop, after which an ear defining sound of laughter and mocking followed. Are you crazy? I can't imagine taking orders from an asshole, and so on...

...Finally the meeting was closed without coming to a conclusion. But the asshole, shocked by the events decided to instantly stop all shit from passing through. Days, weeks and months passed by when the brain started having pains, the eyes not able to see clearly, the hart skipping beats and the legs not able to carry weight. At this point all parts of the body in some way was affected. Everyone started to

wonder what is going on. But after a quick check it became clear that the problems were caused because the asshole was not letting shit pass through. A delegate was formed to talk to the asshole and out of fear it was decided that the asshole should become the new boss.

This story illustrates how any asshole can be the boss!"

The writer is unknown to me, and the exact wording I do not remember, but I assume that the original text was written as a joke.

However, for me this story illustrates much more. I see similarity between this story and the way knowledge interacts with imagination, but also how people, groups of people, countries and regions interact, as if they are not all part of the same thing, each with their own individual tasks and responsibilities that go with these tasks.

Yes, knowledge is important but so is imagination.

And whatever process both must pass through, there is always the final step that both must make for anything to become of them. I am convinced that you need to believe in what you've imagined or what you know before you can use either.

1.1.5 The power of believing; everything is possible.

If you do not believe in what you've imagined, then what you've imagined will remain nothing more than an un-manifested image.

If you do not believe in what you know then you cannot use it effectively. This makes both, what you've imagined and your knowledge worthless.

Now we have two important tools constantly waging war against each other for the attention of belief. Both hopeful that belief will ignite the hidden power that lies within. Imagine how it could be if you believed that these two powerful tools, in harmony, together take care of your needs.

This is the kind of power I'm talking about, the power that makes everything possible. And, do you know what the funny thing is? It's all up to you. Yes you!

To unlock these enormous powers you must choose to be one with yourself. And in your communications be conscious of the different frequencies you can tune in to. When you adjust to the right frequency it will allow you to understand everything that is needed to achieve your ultimate goals.

I know this sounds a bit philosophical or maybe even spiritual, but it's not meant to be. I mean it in the most practical way possible.

Consider that this journey that you and I started once we took our first breath of air is a journey of inspiration and realization. And CARE is designed to take you through all of the steps to get you there. However, it's up to you to CARE effectively and at the right time.

Have you noticed that since you started this journey called life you are constantly pushed, pulled, screamed at, molested and all other attempts have been made with only one and the same purpose of getting you to believe in someone or something?

Think about it. Go to the store and buy anything. Notice that 80%, if not more of the price you just paid went into campaigns asking you to believe in that product or the company that sold it to you. Every few years politicians go into a spending spree and scream for you to believe in them. Even in this book I am asking you to believe in someone and something. No, I'm not asking you to believe in me but yes I am asking you to believe in you and the fact that you are able to CARE in a way that can make your dreams come true.

The hunt for your belief has been going on from the moment humans became conscious of consciousness and is now at its highest peak. This should make it clear to you how valuable you are. You are the sole owner of your ability to believe! This means that no one else but you can determine your value and if you choose to believe that everything is possible then you will find a way to make it happen.

You too can make a difference, not only in your own life but also in the lives of others. Just like Orville and Wilbur Wright who made it possible for humans to fly or Mohammad Yanus, who developed the concept of microcredit enabling the poorest of the poor to some extent take charge of their own lives and not to mention Sir Isaac Newton or Albert Einstein, both considered to be among the greatest minds of all times.

Imagine the power you have at your disposal and all you need to do to activate this power is to be conscious of every single choice you make. But most of all, whatever you choose to imagine or to know, make sure that you are ready to accept all consequences thereof and the choice must be yours.

Yes, great power comes with great responsibility; it is therefore essential that you take this responsibility seriously and find the right balance. To unleash the enormous power to create, live, explore and genuinely be you is not a one-time event. It is an ongoing process that takes place every day, hour, minute, second or fraction thereof.

To tap into this endless field of possibilities and to engage in this effortless process of creation all you need to do is take the first simple step;

Just imagine it!

1.1.6 How to imagine

There are different ways to use your imagination like meditation, chi gong, yoga and visualization. In the following part of Bridge to Success I will discuss the basics of creative visualization in its simplest form. You can apply this simple technique to increase the effect of your imagination process. This technique is not new, but nevertheless, if it is applied correctly, it is very effective.

> *Creative Visualization:*
>
> Care, attention and full relaxation are vital elements to any successful imagination process. This is why you select a goal you care about to start the process of creative

visualization. Then commit yourself to pay the attention that is needed to get you in a relaxed state of mind. The goal you choose could be anything; for instance something you want to have; a car, a home, a caring wife or husband etc., a situation you want to be in, like a beauty pageant, song contest, helping someone or something you would like to improve about yourself. It is important that you are as specific as possible about the goal you choose.

The next step is to choose the surroundings in which you can be totally focused without interruptions. In fact the best time to do Creative Visualization is in bed just before you fall asleep or in the morning just before you fully awaken.

These moments when you are half asleep and half awake are the moments when you are fully relaxed and the interaction between your conscious and unconscious mind is the most active. It is the time when your reticular formation or internal antennea is at high alert.

'The reticular formation is a part of the brain that is involved in actions such as awaking/sleeping cycle, and filtering incoming stimuli to discriminate irrelevant background stimuli. It is essential for governing some of the basic functions

of higher organisms, and is one of the phylogenetically oldest portions of the brain."

If possible repeat the process one more time during the day. And make sure that whenever you do it you are totally relaxed, in a comfortable position and in a quiet place where there are no distractions.

Now focus on your body. Start with your toes and go up to the top of your head. With every step, feel what is taking place in the part you are focused on and release the tension. Breathe deeply and slowly, feel the air filling your lungs and going deeper and deeper until it reaches 7 to 8 cm under your belly button and change direction coming back up slowly and leaving your body. Count down slowly from ten to zero, with each count feel yourself relax deeper and deeper.

When there is no sign of discomfort and you feel deeply relaxed, start to imagine your goal. Use all your senses and be specific about all details as you see the surroundings, objects and people, smell the scent, hear the sounds, feel the emotions and know that everything you feel, smell and hear is true. Make sure you are thorough, but more important have fun and take as much time as you need to enjoy this moment to the fullest.

While you keep the idea or image alive in your mind make some positive statements to yourself mentally. You can do this silently or aloud, whichever you prefer. These positive statements, called affirmations, are a very important part of Creative Visualization. They can sound anything like this:

- My music makes the crowd go wild, and I love it.
- I'm so beautiful, this crown fits me perfectly.
- This is a perfect spot for the swimming pool in my new back yard.

The Visualization process can take 5 minutes or half an hour, this is up to you. The only requirement is that you must enjoy it.

1.2 Decide to do what is needed to grow your thoughts into reality.

Remember, earlier I mentioned the struggle between knowledge and imagination? During your lifetime this struggle to keep you within your comfort zone takes place continually, and, as you will notice further on in this book, it also takes place on different levels of your existence. In some cases it's a mild struggle and in others a full blown war.

Whenever it takes place 95% of your attention is kept occupied with either matters within yourself or matters concerning situations in the past. This will leave only 5% of your attention free to spend consciously in the moment of now to make decisions or take actions that can take you where you want to go.

Let us take a look at the process of Creative Visualization. Here, this struggle can start when doubts and contradictory thoughts arise. The most natural response will be to resist or to push them away. But this will only create the perfect feeding ground for these doubts and contradictory thoughts to gain strength and fight back. As a result, the relaxed state that is needed to effectively visualize will be replaced by tension in your body. Your focus will shift from your goals and the images produced to the discomfort caused by these tensions in your muscles. Ultimately you will slowly but surely wind up pre-occupied with everything else but Creative Visualization. I believe the name for this process should be EGO (Everything else but GO).

Before you reach this point you must **decide**; do I allow my Ego to take charge and start the fight in an attempt to hold on to what I know or do I allow the unknown to become known. The decision you make will always have more than one dimension.

For example, should you decide to resist or to push away the doubts and contradictory thoughts, then in fact you choose to fight. Moreover, you will then have automatically chosen for whatever comes after the fight, if ever this war comes to a conclusion. The problem here is that you do not know what to expect and when to expect it. As a result, many people choose to take no action and end up their whole life waiting and making smaller contribution to life than they would have liked.

It is like starting a feud and having it go on for generations while nobody knows what started it in the first place. Tradition won't allow you to do anything else than fight because this is what you know best. As no kind of communication seems possible, you will spend 95% of your attention waiting, until the enemy makes a move and planning how to react when they finally do.

I remember a conversation with Sarah, my six year old daughter. Even though at this age she could speak clearly and explain her thoughts very well, she sometimes had mood swings and it was difficult for her to talk about her feelings. So I told her not to be too harsh on herself and with time she would learn to understand and cope. But for now pay attention to what happens when she feels a change is taking place in her mood and by looking closely she will learn to know herself better. Before I could finish my sentence she turned to me and said; but dad this means that there must be two of me. I was very surprised by her response so I asked her what she meant.

She replied: 'if I am to know myself then there must be one knowing the other. So if I am the one to know myself then is myself not the one who is being known? Doesn't this make two of me?' I was amazed by this thorough analysis from my little Sarah.

In my view she is completely correct to come to this conclusion and I believe that the same question also applies to this situation; is imagination the enemy or are knowledge, doubt and contradictory thoughts the enemy and which one is you?

So in fact, as long as you allow there to be an enemy, you allow yourself to be incomplete and consistently at war. Perhaps this is why there are so many people looking for themselves, feeling lost, feeling as though they don't belong or any other form of not being able to be who they really are.

Again this has to do with using 95% of your attention waging a war that can only bring destruction. And if it is your intention to engage in self destruction, then by all means continue to do so. You are free to choose, but please do not forget to accept responsibility for all consequences. However, should your intentions be anything other than self destruction, then I propose you embrace the doubts and contradictory thoughts and let them flow through your consciousness. Acknowledge them! Allow yourself to be one with yourself and return 100% of your care and attention to your positive goals and your power of imagination. This is how you create unity and enable all aspects of youself to work as one towards your common goals.

1.2.1 Idea in action

Allow me to tell you a story to illustrate in a simple way the interaction that takes place when deciding to do what is needed to grow your thoughts into reality.

In this example you will see how IDEA is put into practice, daily in its simplest form.

It was in the late nineteen sixties in Aruba where I was born and grew up. I guess I was seven or eight years old, every day walking to and from school. The freedom I enjoyed being able to choose; do I go right, left or straight ahead? I assume it was the inquisitive side of me in search of new things to experience that caused me to try a different road each time. Instead of going home directly from school I often choose to visit friends or family, where I could spend some time playing. Fortunately for me it was a time where the possibility still existed to enjoy this kind of freedom without the threat of being attacked, molested or kidnapped. However, kidnapping would have been a dumb mistake as my parents had next to no money. We were actually financially poor. Seeing my mother struggle hard every day to make ends meet, then, raising seven boys and one little girl, I often wondered how is it possible that life could be this hard for this one person who needs to take care of all of my brothers and sister. I often thought of ways to help, but never got far. But still, I guess, thinking about it meant that I already decided to help, but at that moment I didn't know how.

However, one day as I walked from school with a couple of friends on our way through the village, my attention was caught by a boy, not older than twelve or thirteen. He was carrying the groceries for a lady and as he put the bags in her car the lady thanked him and gave him some money. About two weeks later I noticed that for the last two weeks I, not only going to, but also from school, took the same road. Every time National supermarket was in sight I began to have some kind of nervous reaction.

In retrospect I now understand that my intention of wanting to help my mother was communicating with me, asking me to imagine the possibility of doing the same I saw that boy doing two weeks earlier. And as you may understand, my imagination process kicked in heavily. It cost me a next two weeks before I made the decision to walk into the supermarket and ask the owner for a job. But this was merely the first step. After the Chinese owner said yes and laid out the rules, including punishments for making mistakes and the fact that my parents needed to give their consent, I now had to convince my mom to allow me to do this job, every day after school. Actually it was a lousy paying job. My salary would be about one U$ dollar per week for making sure the shelves are well stocked at all times, pricing the products and putting the client's groceries into bags and boxes and helping them to put it into the car. So why did I still make the effort to convince my mom to allow me to work?

Even though I was only eight years old, I did not expect to earn only one dollar a week, I saw the hidden opportunities and so I went back and revisited my imagination process. This time the focus was on how much I could expect to earn as a result of the kindness of clients and how I personally could influence how much tips I would receive. Once I was ok with the possibilities, I decided to get my mother's permission.

Because, as small as I was, I understood what I saw about a month earlier, and I expected that part of the job to become my cash cow. So after about a month of doing the job I analyzed the results and realized that what I had unconsciously decided to achieve, through this job, was going pretty well. On the Friday evening and Saturday alone I earned about forty U$ dollars. For an eight year old child in the late nineteen sixties that was a lot of money. And every cent of it could definitely be used to help feed the family. Besides, this is how I became my mom's right hand and I was happy with the chance for me to meet with and help lots of new people.

Even though the greater part of this process took place unconsciously, let's recap and see how IDEA was put into effect; under the guidance of intention, which I will discuss later in more details, I imagined not only working at the supermarket but also what to do to get the job. Eventually I made the decision to do what was necessary to get the job. Once I was confronted with the possibility of my expectations with regard to earning enough to help my Mom not being met with, I revisited the imagination process and saw other options which could solve that potential problem. After a month I analyzed the situation and understood that what was created was to my satisfaction. And all it took to start this process of creation was an IDEA, the power of Imagination and the decision to make it happen.

1.3 Allow your expectations to exceed your imaginative potential.

Now you know how to use your imagination to create options. You also know how to make the decision to do what is needed to grow your thoughts into reality. But as you explore the vast amounts of actions to be taken you get a glimpse at possible results as a consequence of taking these actions. So you ask yourself: is this what I expected?

Notice that at this point no action has been taken, only the thought of an action. But still, when you see the possible outcome of an action and this does not meet with your expectations you are inclined to take a step back and change your decision. Is it not strange to see that once again you are invited to go around in circles at one of life's roundabouts? It seems like EGO (anything else but go) has many faces, doesn't it?

However, his/her actions follow a specific pattern; doubt is injected into the process you are engaged in, and once this doubt takes root you are invited to enter into a continuous loop of going around in circles. But why is this? I find this a very interesting question to which part of the answer is to keep you safe within your comfort zone. But why is it important for us to remain within our comfort zone? I will give an answer to this question along the way.

But now it is essential that you understand how important this phase is in the process of creation. This is when the bridge is built between the mental and the physical manifestation of your IDEA.

1.3.1 Bridge to physical manifestation of your idea.

To understand what I mean let me take you through some examples;

She was ordered to appear for her trial on December 5th, 1955. Did she expect this to happen when she refused to obey the law and surrender her seat to a white person? Probably yes, but did Rosa Parks also expect that from that moment she would become famous, and in 1987, establish the Rosa and Raymond Parks Institute for Self- Development to improve the lives of black children. And she ultimately received two of the, United States of America's highest honors for her civil rights activism. In 1996, President Clinton honored her with the Presidential Medal of Freedom. And in 1999, she received the Congressional Gold Medal of Honor.

"During the segregation of the nineteen fifties Rosa Parks and three other black people were seated in the middle area of the bus when a white person got on the bus and wanted a seat. The bus driver demanded that all four black people leave their seats so the white person would not have to sit next to any of them. The three other blacks got up, but Miss Parks refused. As then, in much of the American South the first rows of seats on city buses were for white people only. Black people were restricted to sit in the back of the bus. In a middle area both groups could sit, however black people sitting in that part of the bus were expected to leave their seats if a white person wanted to sit there. And as she refused Rosa Parks was arrested.

This was not the first time that a black person refused to give up a seat on the bus to a white person. In previous occasions blacks had been arrested and even killed for violating orders from bus drivers. However, this one event prompted Martin Luther King Junior to seize the moment and he organized The Montgomery bus boycott. And subsequently similar protests were held in other southern cities. Finally, about one year later on November thirteenth, nineteen fifty-six, the Supreme Court of the United States ruled on Miss Parks's case. It made racial separation illegal on city buses.

Rosa Parks and Martin Luther King, Junior had started a movement of non- violent protest in the South. That movement changed civil rights in the

United States forever. Martin Luther King became its famous spokesman, but he did not live to see many of the results of his work. Rosa Parks did.

But the question still remains; what did Rosa Parks expect to become of her refusal to give up that bus seat to a white person? I do not know the answer to this question. However, when you take a close look at the situation at that time it would be safe to say that chances for positive things to come from this one refusal were next to nothing.

In those days, black people were being mistreated in all possible ways. The laws were aimed at maintaining the status quo; suppression of blacks, they were arrested and even killed for refusing to give up a seat in the bus to a white person. In fact Rosa Parks and her family's lives became increasingly difficult after the bus boycott. She was dismissed from her job and could not find another. So she and her family left Montgomery. First they moved to Virginia, then to Detroit, Michigan where she worked as a seamstress until 1965. I wonder what Rosa Parks's expectations were at the moment she said no; this is enough, and how these expectations evolved in time.

1.3.2 In control of expectations.

Did you notice while reading this example that expectations are flexible? We adapt what we expect to circumstances, the meaning we give to these circumstances and how they evolve. There are yet a few examples I will share with you, but this time the question is not what you expect for or from yourself, but what other people expect of you or you from other people.

In 1961 a boy was born in the eastern part of the Moroccan mountains where he lived between cows, donkeys and lots of stones and he drank water from water wells until he moved to The Netherlands. I'm sure, like it is for the most of us, it is difficult for you to imagine, while you see him playing as a child on the streets of Amsterdam, to expect that Ahmed Aboutaleb would become the first Moroccan born mayor of Rotterdam.

And a boy who was also born in 1961 when racial tensions in America where sky high. His father was a black African and his mother a white American. He became victim to a broken home as his parents divorced when he was only two years old. While seeing him as a nine year old play in the streets of Indonesia, where he lived a good part of his childhood, could you have expected Barack Obama to become the first black president of The United States of America?

I seriously doubt it. So what made this outcome possible?

1.3.3 Expectations; detours from life's highway.

Expectations tend to divert us from life's highway into secondary and country side roads. While these roads offer a pleasant drive where we can slow down, enjoy the scenery, take fresh breaths of air and recharge our batteries, we often get lost in that state of mind and cannot find our way back to the highway that leads us to our destination. Should you, while in this state of mind, accept that this is what you've imagined, it meets with your expectations and then consciously decide to continue doing it, you will have reached the road leading you to your destination.

I must make it clear that highway, secondary and country roads in my examples do not differ in quality. As there are many roads that lead to Rome, secondary and country roads can get you to your destination besides the highway.

However, as long as there remains tension and a feeling of inner conflict, you must find your way back to the highway. Maybe the next detour will be yours to follow. But first find your way back. This is essential and each time you hurry back to find the highway, always take with you the beautiful experiences and impressions, you encountered while away from the highway.

1.3.4 First step into the unknown.

It was May 30th 1979, as I stepped into the airplane, for the first time, on my way to The Netherlands, where I was to start my studies. I was alone, just eighteen years old and for the first time in my life put on an airplane, a one-way ticket to a country far away. And even though I had heard stories about how cold it could be I never imagined what this meant.

On our stopover in Portugal, passengers were allowed to leave the plane. And as I stepped out of the aircraft I could see the air that I breathed become smoke in front of me. It was going on to eight o'clock in the evening and the sun was shining brightly, but still it was in my experience freezing cold, fifteen or sixteen degrees Celsius. Eight o' clock in the evening and the sun shining brightly for me was something unbelievable. As I was accustomed to high temperatures of twenty nine or thirty degrees Celsius the whole year around I asked myself: what the heck is going on? Here I am standing outside in the open air, the sun is shining, touching my face and I feel no warmth at all. How is this possible, I asked myself and at that moment the only logical conclusion I could come up with was "Air-conditioning", eureka!

But wait, air-conditioning outside, who is foolish enough to spend so much money on electricity to install air-conditioning in the open air? Yes, this is how naïve I was in those days.

It wasn't until I landed in Amsterdam, that my brother, Reggy and his friends, while driving me to my new home, from the Airport and after having their laughs, explained the weather situation to me. I understood, at least I thought I understood until my first winter experience, when I finally found out what freezing cold really was.

You see the circumstances changed: unprepared I entered into a world completely unknown to me while I built my expectations based on the situation I left behind.

This became even clearer to me about a week later, when I was taking a ride on a scooter I borrowed from one of my friends' girlfriend. Reggy and friends were practicing music with their reggae band "The Lord of Lords" and I decided to explore the area to get a sense of where I was and how to find my whereabouts. I was amazed to see people live in huge complexes called flats or apartment buildings. In my mind the only people who stayed in these kinds of buildings, known to me as hotels were tourists.

How fast people moved to go from one place to another, not taking time to notice their surroundings or to kindly greet people on the streets was also new to me. And as I cruised along on the bicycle lane, deeply in thought, there was a steep piece of road going into a curb, but the curb was not visible until you reached the top of the road. However, as I reached the top, instead of going with the curb I went straight ahead and landed into a ditch. This was so dirty, I spontaneously started itching and all kind of red marks and bumps covered the surface of my skin.

As I stood in this ditch, alone in the middle of nowhere, with tears in my eyes I saw a lady on her bicycle approach. In Aruba, a small Island in the Caribbean where everyone knows their neighbours I could expect that this lady, of between thirty five or forty years old, would be kind and try to help me. So I was a bit relieved to see this person approach hoping that some

CARE was on the way. To my surprise this lady acted as though she knew me.

Instead of showing CARE she, while riding on her bike, looks at me and shouts these words; good for you, you stinking nigger, it's a pity you didn't drown.

This event shocked me deep into the core of my existence and I decided there and then not to ever allow circumstances to dictate what to expect.

Events like this, in one way or another, take place every day all over the world promting people like you and me to make choices. Even though these events are very compelling, understand that they can only compel you to make a choice. They can never compel you what to choose.

1.3.5 How to neutralize deflection.

Ask yourself; to what extent can you influence circumstances, your behavior, the behavior of your friends, strangers, family, parents or your own mind set.

In answer to the question how to neutralize deflection you must understand that circumstances and people (including your parents) are what they are. And as long as you do not accept this, you in fact choose not to get on with your life and invest time and energy trying to change them. But do you realize that trying to change them is often experienced as rejection and therefore a direct attack on their right to exist?

Indirectly what you are doing is forcing others to make use of your compass and by doing so telling them their compass is trash and should be thrown away. Doesn't this seem like making enemies? Of course, this all takes place in your unconscious mind and therefore, unconsciously they become your enemy.

As you know, having enemies means spending 95% of your care and attention on doing everything else but GO.

Make no mistake about this; everywhere you are your enemies will be there too. They will continually have you sabotage yourself and cause short circuits in your body's electrical system. As a result you will have all kinds of anxiety attacks, physical discomfort, headaches, stomach aches, depressions and all kinds of problems. You will seek comfort in different sorts of excessive habits like; eating, drinking, smoking, biting nails, sex and others. Later on in this book I will explain how to address these issues should you, in first instance, choose to have these enemies.

By now you should understand that the only thing worth influencing is your own mind set. You can start doing this by making the choice right now to accept and embrace the circumstances and people that caused you a moment of disbelief.

Have you noticed I did not use the word pain or discomfort? The reason for this is that by calling it pain or discomfort instead of disbelief I add a specific value to the circumstance or person's action. By doing this when you think of this situation or person's action you will experience pain or discomfort. And how hard is it for you to, willingly, accept and embrace pain and discomfort? Wouldn't you agree that this is difficult?

However, by calling it disbelief a window of opportunity opens for you to use your imagination and give different meaning to the situation or a person's action that you are willing to accept and embrace, while you get on with your life.

1.3.6 Why do we remain within our comfort zone?

Humans experience risks as an attack on our existence. It is our intrinsic task to survive and therefore we automatically behave in ways that will keep us away from risks of any kind at any level. Via behavioral patterns we create an unfounded sense of security by conditioning ourselves mentally and creating mental boundaries which will cause alarm bells to go off any time we try to cross these boundaries. This is the same mechanism as I discussed earlier with regard to the struggle between imagination and knowledge. What I did not mention before, but you might have guessed, is that once the alarm bells go off, EGO sends troops of anxiety to force us back.

The size of our comfort zones and boundaries is not the same for every person, but there are large groups of people who behave in the same way when in a similar situation. Today, there are many personality tests to determine what type of person you are and how you most probably will respond to certain occurrences while in a specific environment. Most of these tests are used by human resource departments at large companies to find the perfect fit between the company and potential new employees. Or to apply tailor made personal development programs for existing employees. One of the most used personality type tests is the Myers-Briggs Type Indicator, MBTI. This psychometric questionnaire was designed by Katharine Cook Briggs and her daughter, Isabel Briggs Myers, to measure psychological preferences in how people perceive the world and make decisions. These preferences were extrapolated from the typological theories originated by Carl Gustav Jung, as published in his 1921 book Psychological Types.

The Myers-Briggs typology model regards personality type as similar to left or right handedness: individuals are either born with, or develop, certain preferred ways of thinking and acting. The MBTI sorts some of these psychological differences into four opposite pairs, or dichotomies, with a resulting 16 possible psychological types. None of these types is "better" or "worse"; however, Briggs and Myers theorized that individuals naturally prefer one overall combination of type differences. In the same way that writing with the left hand is hard work for a right-handed person, so people tend to find using their opposite psychological preferences more difficult, even if they can become more proficient (and therefore behaviorally flexible) with practice and development.

The 16 different types are often referred to by an abreviation of four letters, the initial letters of each of their four type preferences (except in the case of iNtuition, which uses N to distinguish it from Introversion). For instance:

ESTJ - Extraversion, Sensing, Thinking, Judging.

INFP - Introversion, iNtuition, Feeling, Perceiving.

And so on for all 16 possible type combinations.

In fact all personality type tests are based on the same principles as the MBTI. The result is sets of preferred behavior in response to a given situation.

Now ask yourself if preferred behavior means you have the opportunity to choose your behavior. If indeed situations offer you possibilities to choose from, then the next interesting questions to be answered are; what makes your preferred behavior the most obvious choice and what criteria do you use to determine this behavior?

I want to take you back to 1979; that young boy freshly sent out into the unknown, to meet the world. All alone in the middle of nowhere, standing in a filthy ditch with tears in his eyes, expecting some kind of care from a stranger and receiving hostility instead.

Remember, earlier I mentioned how compelling these events are, and never the less they cannot compel you which choice to make. On a conscious level this is 100% true, but unconsciously the emotions you experience and the meaning you give to these emotions will remain with you and form part of your boundaries. This is why you allow your EGO to station anxiety to guard the boundaries, and keep you imprisoned within your comfort zone.

This is one event but in your lifetime I'm sure there are thousands of situations and people who in the past and now still consciously or unconsciously cause you to form your expectations. This is done through the meaning you give to emotions you experience. Previously I explained what my conscious reaction to this one situation was. In part two of Bridge to Success I will tell you what happened to me unconsciously, on an emotional level. But now let us take a look at how this process evolves.

1.3.7 Writing on the wall.

As I struggle to find a simple way to explain the concept of comfort zone, self imprisonment and the belief system and how this evolves, I decided to take a break. While still in thoughts, walking from my office to the living room, where I thought my wife was alone I heard a male voice speaking. As I entered into the room I saw my wife sitting on the couch staring in front of her as she taps the top of her head, while this person talks about a palace of possibilities. As my curiosity rose I walked over to my wife and sat beside her on the couch to watch the remaining part of the series of EFT DVD's we were studying for some time. According to the founder, Gary Craig;

"EFT is a powerful new discovery that combines two well established sciences so you can benefit from both at the same time:

1. *Mind Body Medicine*
2. *Acupuncture (without needles).*

In essence, EFT is an emotional version of acupuncture wherein we stimulate certain meridian points by tapping on them with our fingertips. This addresses a new cause for emotional issues (unbalanced energy meridians). Properly done, this frequently reduces the therapeutic process from months or years down to hours or minutes. And, since emotional stress can contribute to pain, disease and physical ailments, we often find that EFT provides astonishing physical relief".

However, all the time Mirjam and I were studying and testing this new technique with the intention to use it to help our clients even better, this was the first time I heard Gary Craig talk about the Palace of Possibilities. To cut a long story short; I found myself sitting next to Mirjam listening to Gary talk about Palace of Possibilities and this was exactly what I needed at that moment. Also, remember in my introduction I mentioned that I consistently receive everything I need; this is one of the many perfect examples of what I meant and how this works.

Now I can share with you what my views are on comfort zones, self imprisonment and the belief system by use of Gary's wording, without having to struggle any further.

"We live in a palace of possibilities, which is a metaphor for saying we have far more potential than we are using. Even though this piece of information is nothing new, this example will be easy to understand. Because the palace of possibilities represents all of our potential, it's filled with joyous rooms, rooms of abundance, successes, achievement and everything else we want. Maybe we deserve to be in those rooms, maybe we should be there and maybe we could belong in there. However, what we tend to do is stay in our own room which is in fact our own comfort zones. Because other people occupy those rooms, richer people, better connected people, luckier people, and people with more talent, people that are smarter or whatever the reason may be. Those rooms are for other people, I don't quite belong there; besides, I have my own room, my comfort zone.

The interesting thing about my room is that it has walls and the walls have writing on them that I read every day. These walls are filled with what I can and cannot do, what I should or should not do and what I must or must not do. All my beliefs, my attitudes, all my experiences and everything that has come to be the truth to me are written on my walls, and I see them all the time. So if I'm going to do something new, step out of my room I might read my walls and they say: no, no, no, you can't do that, that's for other people to do. If you do that, you will feel uncomfortable or you don't have any experience with that. Or your mother, she's going to get on you if you do that and so on. These are very powerful writings on our walls. The writings on our walls to me are the same as our expectations".

Now this is how your expectations or writings on your walls build the bridge between the mental and the physical manifestation of your IDEAS.

Having thoughts is a mental process that is fed by expectations, which are writings on your walls. The physical manifestation of this mental process occurs when these consistent thoughts become your reality or truth. Every hour, minute, second or parts thereof, the writings on your walls are consulted before you make any decision or take any action. This process takes place in a split second and maybe that is why we take it for granted. So how is it possible that we do not question the origins of these writings and we allow this process, which is as important as taking a breath of air to become something we take for granted?

1.3.8 Where do expectations come from

My ditch incident is a perfect example of something being written on my walls because of my encounter with a complete stranger. But there are many more people constantly having us writing things on our walls. Think about parents, friends, teachers, uncles, aunts, religions, colleagues, bosses, TV, radio, newspapers, magazines, books, movies, even perfect strangers and all of our experiences.

Parents do a lot of writing on our walls; just think for a while about your mother or father, the sentences or words they use to correct you, stimulate you or to protect you from danger. Actually, it doesn't matter what they said or the intention with which they said it. The meaning you gave to these sentences is what you use to determine what to expect and that is what you have written on your walls.

Things like 'be careful child', 'don't do that', 'it's dangerous', 'clean your plate', 'children should be seen and not heard', 'A woman's place is in the kitchen', 'don't talk back', 'daddy's little girl', 'no pain no gain', 'mommy's little boy', 'do this or else' or 'don't do that or else' etc. Beside the words used, actions also contribute to writings on our walls and I'm sure you can come up with something you heard or saw your mother, father, sibling, friends and so on say or do so often; it causes you even today to go into automatic mode whenever you are triggered to react.

1.3.9 Poor little Nick.

Once a week, in the mornings when I take my daughter to kinder garten I sometimes see Nick, who is a little boy of three, enthusiastically sit next to my Louise and pick a puzzle to play with.

As Nick starts to play with the puzzle his mother takes the puzzle away and replaces it with another one. Nick, of course always protests and his mother every time says; take this one it's easy, you cannot do the other one, because it's too difficult. Every time I see this happen, I am amazed and wonder if this person knows what the long term effect of this behavior most probably will be?

Does she realize that saying this to her child frequently is the same as programming Nick according to her beliefs? And in fact she is writing on Nick's walls what he should expect of himself and the world?

Is this a conscious act and where does it come from? Is it her intention to protect or to limit her child in his abilities? The most important question is what meaning will Nick give to this message?

One day as I sat next to Louise I saw Nick come into the class room. That day he was not with his mother but his grandmother, who brought him to school that day. By then I already had the routine between Nick and his mom written all over my walls and so I expected to be spared that routine this time. I thought wow; hopefully today Nick will finally be able to do the puzzle he has been trying to get his hands on for so long.

I was wrong; the movie was exactly the same; the supporting actor was different. Poor Nick I thought, his grandmother was even more convincing with her plea that Nick could not do this puzzle. It was a puzzle that Livy, Louise and more three year olds had already done for the past 3 months.

Is this a family tradition, where did it start and where will it end?

This is a classic example of how while we care for our children, even with the best of intentions in the world we allow the unresolved issues of our past (*I spoke about earlier; the feud that nobody knows what started it*) to capture our full attention. We lose focus of the care we try to give to our children and the attention that goes with that CARE.

By allowing this to happen we end up, instead of putting care into the wellbeing of our children, putting care into the struggle we have with these unresolved issues. This is how we keep the struggle alive.

You see, CARE is expressed through attention. So if it is your intention to care for your child, then you must pay attention to the wellbeing of your child and allow yourself to be free from your own limitations.

Do not allow past issues to push you into automatic mode and cause you to follow standard patterns.

Even though you believe that you follow these patterns in the name of love, to protect your child, be aware that you will be pushing your child away from finding his/her own path into following yours. But this time hopefully under your protection. This will only make your child dependent on you.

1.4 Analyze your point of origin in relation to your destination.

Often when asked, what the cause or where the starting point of a process is we automatically look into the past in search for the answers. Take a look at poor little Nick's Wednesday morning puzzle routine.

Logic would suggest that what Nick is being taught to expect from himself comes directly from his mother, his grandmother and indirectly from their parents and grandparents.

However, there will come a point in his life when Nick must determine how far back in time he should trace his roots to find the starting point leading him to his destination. His decision in this matter will determine how much responsibility he wants to accept to create his own history.

A few months ago Daniël at the Freemasons Lodge asked if I expect him to apologize to me for all of the sufferings imposed on blacks during slavery. My response was; as long as you do not consider me to be your slave, it is not your intention to mistreat me as if you are my master and you show the same respect as you would expect from me, then I see no reason why you should apologize to me.

Even though the question puzzled me I understood where he was coming from. It is the question about taking responsibility for who I am and who I want to be. The same question Nick and every other person will eventually have to answer when he or she grows up.

I personally know people who often use the effects of this period, when blacks where bought, sold and enslaved, to justify certain behavior. But is it logical for a black person, living in hardship in the ghetto's of New York, London, Paris, Frankfurt or Amsterdam to hold on to this idea; more than four hundred years of slavery is the cause of my misfortune today?

It is conceivable that there are emotional issues that can be triggered through the way races today interact with each other. However, is it not logical to assume that the distance between your success and the starting point of your journey will be increased by a few centuries if you choose the starting point of your journey to success to be your forefathers' experiences as a slave?

1.4.1 Where are you now?

Now, think about the relationships you have with others for example; parents, grandparents, sibling, other family, friends, schoolmates, business colleagues, your community, fellow citizens etc…

Then imagine that all people are like you travelers on the same journey of life. Occasionally your paths cross and you build one or more relationships. Do you realize that the type of relationship you have with any human being, including yourself is determined only by the present moment? I'm not talking about the name of the relationships like father, mother, brother, sister, friend, colleague etc… What I'm saying is that every moment that is present, the care you put into each relationship will determine the meaning you give to that relationship with other people but also with yourself.

Once you realize this you will come to understand how important it is to always choose this moment as your starting point. Because in fact this moment is all you have, yesterday is gone and tomorrow is waiting for you to decide right now, what you want it to bring. This is why your point of origin is always now.

Ask yourself, where am I at this moment in life and look into the past for the answer. There is 99, 9% chance you will not find the answer in the past. The most probable place to look is where you are right now, at this moment.

I could imagine, this sounds a bit strange however, I am sure that the only place to find where you are is right here, right now, where you are at this moment and nowhere else.

1.4.2 Different perspectives.

The question that now remains is how to look. To answer this question you must take a close look at yourself. Right now, start the process of imagination in search of an idea; preferably far beyond the boundaries of what you know. Be consciously vigilant for any doubts or contradictory thoughts. Whenever you find one, ask yourself; do I acknowledge it, embrace it and let it flow through my consciousness or do I push it away with the risk of starting a self destructive war.

How often you are confronted with this choice, during the process of imagination and the time it takes for you to choose is a good way to determine how willing you are to let go of the past and to accept the present as it presents itself to you. In fact this is an indicator for you to know where you are in life.

You see, by answering these two simple questions you will determine not only where you are but also where you want to be and thus become aware of the distance between where you are and where you want to be.

Remember, in the example I used for Creative Visualizations, doubts and contradictory thoughts sometimes disrupt the process of imagination. Realize that you can only have doubts or contradictory thoughts if, in your perception, there is a discrepancy, between what already exists, what presumably exists and the new thought that has the potential of becoming your new reality.

The present will totally be absorbed by the past and the future as long as you continue to choose to resist and push away these doubts and contradictory thoughts.

You will remain in conflict with yourself and therefore stuck going around in circles at one of the many roundabouts in your life. From the moment you decide to acknowledge and embrace your doubts and the contradictory thoughts, it is safe to say that the attention you otherwise would use to engage in fighting a war will become free. This attention could then be focused on living in the moment. This means that you will better be able to hear what is heard, see what is seen, and feel what is felt and to let go of every impulse you have to add old limiting values to the new possibilities hidden in this moment.

Attention is the key to successfully explore and utilize whatever potentials lay hidden in you at this moment. Once you understand this you will have learned to appreciate the importance of choosing this moment as your point of origin.

1.4.3 Outside the comfort zone.

During the process of creation we often tend to allow our attention to be held captive by the struggle we wage while we try to step out of our comfort zone. There must be something of great value beyond the boundaries of the comfort zone. But what is it, what is outside the comfort zone?

A simple yet accurate answer to the question, what is outside the boundaries of your expectations is; *everything else not inside!*

This is interesting.

Now ask yourself, am I satisfied with, or is everything within my comfort zone enough for me to live a successful life? If the answer is yes then I congratulate you as you are then one of the few to achieve the ultimate goal. But if your answer is no then there is some work to be done to explore beyond these boundaries.

It is common knowledge that highly successful people routinely step outside of the comfort zone to achieve their goals. This makes me wonder why the majority of people do not or have difficulty to freely cross over beyond these boundaries where we know great things are achieved. It seems we get a sense of security, even though it might be false, this feeling is powerful enough to keep us at peace with ourselves. Remember, in chapter one I mentioned, at least 95% of your attention is spent on waging war against your enemies, which in fact is fighting with yourself.

Now that you've conquered five percent of control over your attention, you experience a sense of peace. Imagine five percent instead of none and not even knowing if there is more. Now you can for the first time enjoy the feeling of liberty and freedom of choice. It is logical to experience this victory as a big achievement and to embrace this new found sense of peace with both arms.

1.4.4 What is wrong with the comfort zone?

Actually there is nothing wrong with the comfort zone, as it is designed in support of our survival.

However, ego has taken control and now uses the defensive benefits of the comfort zone to ensure its own survival. Because the ego constitutes only 5% of our human self, our interpretation of survival then becomes ensuring the survival of only this 5%. Hense, to achieve survival we must live within our limited boundaries; to survive we must stay within our comfort zone and anxciety becomes the border patrol tasked to keep us from getting out, while we assume that finding the way to our goals lies beyond the borders of our comfort zone.

I cannot come to any other conclusion; something is wrong, something must be very wrong with our expectations, the role we give to anxiety or both. And as this conclusion emerges the following questions come to mind; how could ego make us believe that beyond these boundaries there is danger? What kind of danger? I wonder, is it that terrible that we expect total extinction? Why does anxiety fulfill the role of border patrol? Can't we formulate a new role for anxiety to fulfill?

Is it possible for us to delete all possibilities of any existence beyond these borders? If we could, would this solve the problem of being curious? What I mean is if we know, believe and can imagine there is nothing beyond these boundaries then we have nothing to look for outside our comfort zone because nothing exists there.

1.4.5 The professional approach.

Later I will address the previous questions but for now look at the situation from a different perspective; the following story I received from my sister in law, Tini about my niece;

"At a very young age our daughter was scouted as an exceptional talent in her field of sport and at age seven joined the national league training. Her talent was noticed by everyone in her surroundings; clubs, coaches, family, friends and colleagues in sport. Many of which complimented her on her achievements, which she gladly accepted, and so she enjoyed the attention.

Her sporting carrier evolved successful; with her team they became national champions, with the Dutch National junior league they won their first international tournament in Italy, with an indoor-cup she won important individual prices, She joined the National selection for the World Championship, and takes part in the selection for the "Koninkrijksspelen" and is often asked by many other teams to join them. And she enjoyed every minute of it.

Now at age fifteen (15) the season did not go completely perfect. As early as the first game Kimberly shed some tears. Coaches and teammates, as they didn't expect this, did not know how to respond and we're helpless in finding the cause. Even with us, her parents, she refused to talk about her emotions. During a following game she froze completely, again tears and no explanation or communication about these emotions. Despite his attempts to talk with her the national coach did not find the reason for her emotional breakdown. Internally Kimberly was silently involved in a heavy struggle which she could not express to others.

One evening as I entered into her room, right before going to sleep, I knew she was vulnerable and so I grabbed my chance to find out what the struggle was about. I told her; Child if the sport is not enjoyable to you anymore, then you can choose to stop! This was enough to get tears flowing and finally she haltingly could explain what was going on inside of her. For some time she imposed such high pressure on herself; she felt everyone knew who Kimberley Jones was, kept a close look on every move she made, many sporting colleagues called her the National Coaches' favorite and when she makes a mistake everyone immediately asks her what is wrong and at trainings she is frequently asked to show the others how a certain exercise needed to be carried out. "Mamma, she said, I wish no one knew me, I want to be invisible, I am not allowed to make mistakes".

This fifteen year old girl in the prime of her youth is struggling with well intended, but still in her experience, imposed expectations of her from others. While all she wants to do is enjoy the sport, have fun to her liking and be happy doing just that.

It is the same in the corporate world where I've seen time and time again people who are blessed with a talent to sell anything and enjoy doing so, are praised to the extent that they are expected to be able to do anything. And even while they are not yet ready to let go of their passion, executive positions are offered to them. As a result they lose the connection with making the sale and end up unhappy wasting their energy reminiscing about the glory days, just surviving from day to day.

I am sure that Kimberly's story, one way or another, sounds familiar to at least 80% of all public figures. Those who became successful and made it to the top in their field of expertise eventually found a way to overcome the pressure of well intended expectations.

Let us take the Spanish tennis star Rafael Nadal, who, I'm sure at some stage of his career, went through the same process as Kimberly. But he found a way to overcome this dilemma. So if he can then Kimberly and everyone else also can. The only question is; how?

In his bestseller "The Inner Game" Timothy Gallwey wrote about Rafael Nadal and his intense focus during the game; here I will take you through this process in three steps:

1. **Look**; during trainings keep your focus on the joints of the ball. After a while you will notice that you can see the ball much better. Besides seeing the ball better absolute focus will prevent distraction by other issues such as the wind, household or work related.

2. **Listen**; pay attention to the sound when the ball hits the racket. The sound will tell you how close to the centre of the racket the ball touched, the angle and the exact spot the ball bounced against the racket. Very soon you will learn to recognize, by the sound when the counter was perfect. Keep this sound in mind, your body will automatically respond aimed at making this sound and thus reproduce that perfect counter.

3. **Feel**; Pay attention to your body. Two things you must know when playing the game of tennis. Where is the ball and where is the racket? Most players know where the ball is, but they forget the racket. Feel where the racket is, how the ball bounced against the racket and where the racket ends up after the counter is essential.

Besides these three steps Nadal enforces his focus with a symbolic routine he built into his game; after every point Nadal asks for three balls. He looks at them thoroughly and gives one back. His socks are set right, his trousers pulled out of his anal cleft, his long hair is tucked away behind his ears. Every time the same ritual, also after the break; with precision he puts down his water bottle and with much care he folds back the banana skin. When back in the field again he asks for three balls. It is as if he uses these rituals to keep him in focus and tap into his higher self.

As you can see, the perfect balance between mind, body and spirit is essential for great things to be achieved. Good communication skills, internal as well as external communication is essential in the process of creating and maintaining the perfect balance.

The purpose of your internal communication process is for you to become one with yourself by obtaining full coherence. To do this effectively, you must live in the moment, erase the past and the future and deal one on one with the present; see what you see, hear what you hear, feel what you feel and be, not what you or anyone else expects you to be, but be who you really are!

1.4.6 Learn by example.

The other day I was talking with my friend Aziz and I heard myself saying that after all these years of helping others I have come to the conclusion that the best way to help others is to help me. This sounds like a selfish thought but actually it's not. You see, it is human nature to learn by example. Within one year from the moment a baby is born it learns to sit, roll, crawl, pull up onto the furniture and stand. In addition it learns within two years how to bend at the knees, sit after standing, stand solo, stop and squat, jump, walk on its own and get up stairs. Beside these physical activities your baby also learns, within these same two years how to talk, listen, smile, and respond to direct questions and much more… What a baby learns in the two first years of its life forms the foundation on which the rest of its life is built. And most of what is learned was done by example. At later ages our children sometimes tend to use the examples we give to do the exact opposite. And even this is learning by example.

So, if I want to help someone be successful, what would be the most effective way for me to do this? Do you think this person will listen to what I have to say if I was not successful? I don't think so.

Now, in this case if you want to help someone be successful, then it is essential for you to be successful yourself. This will make it much easier to help others. Because, when others look at you and follow your examples, the effort you need to put into teaching will be reduced by 50%. It will be reduced by another 30% when this person is really serious about learning and you are genuinely being successful yourself.

What success means to you is personal and cannot be generalized. But whatever it is and whatever qualities are needed to achieve success; honesty, integrity, loyalty, craftsmanship, helpfulness, it doesn't really matter. If you want to help someone else you must see yourself as a role model and possess each and every quality, you want to share, yourself.

1.4.7 CARE in a nutshell, part one.

Before we take the second step in the CARE system lets take one moment to recap;

In part one I discussed the concept of IDEA, how to create your IDEA and the importance of having an IDEA before you can create anything.

I've also discussed different obstacles you may encounter while you create and how to overcome them.

During each of the four steps; *imagine, decide, expect and analyze* there was one consistent element predominantly present and pushing the process forward.

Even though this element was doing its job in silent mode, without it there would be no IDEA to LIVE. Without consciously giving your full attention to and expressing CARE for what you want to create there could be no IDEA and taking the next step to LIVE this IDEA could not be possible.

In figure 1, below you can see that even though 80% of this process consists of internal dialogue it must be followed with great CARE. Whatever

IDEA you come up with will prove to be the foundation on which your life is structured.

You will notice that intention plays an important role within the CARE system. This is why in advance of explaining intention in a later part of this book you will occasionally encounter previews on the power of intention. You will see this happen in the explanation of phase 1 in the following figure 1:

Fig 1.

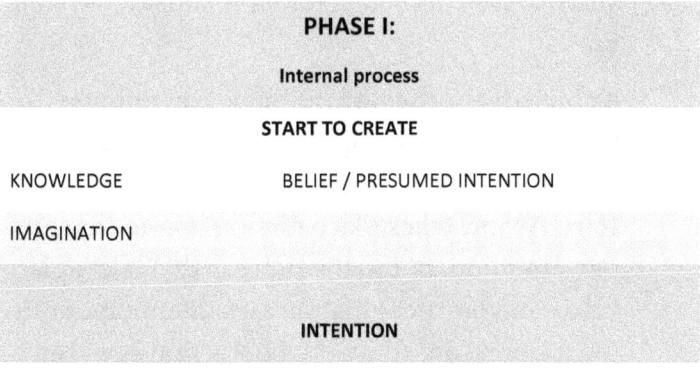

Intention lies at the foundation of everything ever created or yet to be created and acts as the highway throughout all possible stages of existence, ultimately leading to goals.

PHASE I

Intention, and with this I mean the intention of consciousness itself or the entity that created the universe, is the driving force of all you create. However, to tap into and understand what this means for you, you were given the ability to imagine.

This tool; imagination is designed to get you started; building the bridge between formulating an IDEA and the tangible manifestation of this IDEA. But as you know, in this world everything must be tested, checked and double checked before it is considered safe for use.

Knowledge (or what you think you know) is used to do the testing, checking and double checking. This is where the first signs of friction start. A shift takes place forcing you to care and pay attention, not to the process that takes place between your imagination and intention but to the friction caused by the interaction between knowledge and imagination.

But still you must decide to do what is needed, take initiative and analyze the situation before you take the next step. And even when you do decide, your attention remains hostage to the conflicting parties. Eventually you come to a compromise and accept the limitations; by creating a belief which offers comfort. Very often this belief is mistaken for intention and therefore I call it presumed intention.

Eighty percent of this process is an internal process and represents only the starting point of everything you will ever create. Only when you apply the proper care and through your imagination tune into the correct channel you will understand which intention consciousness is communicating to you. And you will effortlessly create whatever is needed to express your true self.

2 Apply

The secret of health for both mind and body is not to mourn for the past, worry about the future, or anticipate troubles, but to live in the present moment wisely and earnestly.

-Buddha-

2.1 Learn by example, take the positive approach.

While I write this book I have come to notice a pattern unfolding. Every time I complete a chapter and start to write the new one I automatically take a pause to consciously consult with my thoughts about the direction to take. Today, September 25th 2009, bridge to success part one is completed and I had been for a greater part of the day in deep thought about where to go from here. The question is not so much what to write but rather how to write it. Later in the evening, as my wife, Mirjam and I were in the car on our way to Amsterdam, to listen to Deepak Chopra's presentation of his new book, *"reinventing the body, resurrecting the soul"*, we discussed the process of thoughts and where they come from. As we talked about the different possibilities we came to the conclusion that thoughts are not present in our minds and maybe not even in our bodies. This might sound like the beginning of a different book however, the reason I share this story with you is because in part one I extensively discussed and came to the conclusion that our constant thoughts become our reality, our belief and our truth. Since thoughts are collections of conscious or unconscious memories, and the way we live our lives is therefore dependent on how we convert not only our thoughts but also these memories through our emotions into actions or behavior. With this in mind my discussion with Mirjam changed from where thoughts come from to where memories come from.

This new question changed my thinking from a philosophical perspective to a practical perspective and eventually we came to the following conclusion. Memories, for centuries have been passed down from generation to generation by word of mouth and writings. But also our genes play an important role in passing down this kind of information. I believe memories, in some way or another are encoded in our body, perhaps packaged into our DNA. During a lifetime this information, or part of it, is released into our nervous system where it is processed into thoughts and linked to emotions.

As these words filled the car I got an aha moment and continued with the following statement; if memories in some way are encoded in DNA, later extracted and used in an internal communication process aimed at producing an action, then it is possible that everything that exists today is made of DNA that was once part of someone or something else in a different time and space. This could mean that answers to the questions about reincarnation could be found, not at the level of humanity, but at a sub-atomic level or the level of DNA.

As we continued our discussion I even made the joke; this means that I am possibly made of parts of Jesus, Mahatma Ghandi, Martin Luther King, and Mother Teresa or maybe even Adolf Hitler. Wow, what a thought.

For the first time ever in my life I had this thought or imagined this concept. Usually this is when EGO sends out the troops to force me back into my comfort zone. However, there was no anxiety, but pure calm, it became quiet in the car and I continued in silence to digest these thoughts.

Ten minutes later we arrived at our destination and as we approached the entrance of the RAI, building a promotional leaflet was given to me with the text; *"Healing with the power of intention"*. I thought; is it coincidence that I just spent the last few weeks writing about intention and the first thing I am confronted with is this message? I did not give it much more attention, as I was preparing myself to be inspired by the teacher, Deepak Chopra.

2.1.1 The lessons learned.

The atmosphere was peaceful, people where relaxed and open to be spoken to and to respond kindly. It was a totally different energy in the air to that of a pop concert, a soccer match or while in the train in the morning or evening when going to or coming from work, when people put up a huge wall to protect them from the outside world without even realizing that at the same time this wall becomes the last parameter of the prison we create to keep our own presumed identity locked up inside.

Mirjam and I sat in our seats in the second row where we had a clear view of our host and we could hear his every word. Not knowing what to expect, a loud applause filled the room while Deepak Chopra made his entrance, after being introduced by a young lady.

Deepak Chopra started his presentation with a series of questions of which one of the first to his public was; do you know where thoughts come from and where they go. As we had just concluded our talks about this question Mirjam and I looked at each other as if we both were experiencing the same déjà vu at that moment. Is this a coincidence?

For me this was the start of a presentation that, contrary to my expectations of being inspired, instead made me feel small. To some degree it even discouraged me from completing this book. There stood the teacher on stage, and while I reflected on myself all I could see was an insignificant little person hungry to learn hungry to teach.

Once again anxiety, the border patrol to my comfort zone was using heavy ammunition to force me back in.

I must say, during the presentation it was difficult to embrace and accept these feelings. But at the end of the presentation something happened. It was as if the universe was reaching out to me with some information that could help me.

2.1.2 Message from the universe.

While the final applause for the evening filled the room for the second time that evening Deepak Chopra was asked to sign books for his audience. He agreed to do so for another twenty minutes. During the previous signing session I already had two books signed and therefore did not need to approach Mister Chopra. But as he climbed down the stage he was immediately surrounded by a huge crowd. This made it difficult for Mirjam and I to get out of the crowd as we sat at the end of the stairs where Deepak Chopra came down the stage.

At a certain moment I heard him ask for a pen, because he had misplaced his. And as he mentioned this, pens from all sides we're put in his face, he accepted one and began to sign books for his fans.

The lady who sat in front of me during the presentation was also one who tried to give her pen to Mr. Chopra. In a joking way I told her in Dutch; you almost succeeded in giving your pen to Deepak Chopra. She looked at me and asked to repeat what I've said in English as she did not understand Dutch. So I did and her response was; no this is Deepak Chopra's own pen I was holding it for him after he did the previous signing session. And as she is saying these words to me I remember seeing her at the beginning of the presentation together with two other people coming from behind the curtains. At this point I assumed that this person was Deepak Chopra's assistant and she is waving his pen in front of me with the question; do you want it, you may have it if you want. And before I could answer she shoved it into my hand and walked away. I didn't even get the chance to thank her. Now could you tell me what this all means? Could this be a coincidence? Is this some kind of sign or what?

Forgive me for once again giving you a preview on intention as I will extensively discuss it later in Bridge to Success. However, it is such an important element at the core of our existence it cannot wait to present itself to you and that is why I now must refer to Deepak Chopra's book "How to know God" where he talked about the 7 qualities that people who have mastered the art of intention posses;

1. They do not attach to the past or possible outcome of a situation.

2. They adapt rapidly to mistakes or bad judgments.

3. They have highly sensitive antennea and notice even the smallest signs.

4. There is a good connection between their spirit and body.

5. They do not have any problems with the acceptance of uncertainty or ambiguity.

6. They patiently await the results of their wishes while fully confident in the universe.

7. They make karmic connections and are able to understand the meaning of coincidental occurrences.

Imagine, within a space of three hours both Mirjam and I we're given the opportunity to test ourselves on all 7 of these qualities. And what does it mean, symbolically, to receive the pen, of this highly enlightened teacher, not only of writing but also of shedding light on life's high way of intention, at a moment when I am in doubt about finishing my book?

This meant, for me that stopping is not an option because to not write this book is the same as not being genuinely me.

But before we continue with building the bridges to your success and for you to understand what I mean, I will share with you some of the insights given to us by Deepak Chopra that evening.

2.1.3 To be conscious of the teachers words.

Deepak Chopra explained perfectly how everything we think, breathe and know is a projection of our consciousness. Everything we are or want to be is pure consciousness and our bodies are constantly renewing itself. Every month different parts of our body like the heart, liver or kidney is completely recycled and new. Every seven years each particle of our whole body has changed and in fact we are a completely new version of ourselves.

Consciousness is everything and it is a mistake to think that consciousness is a part of you because in fact you are a part of consciousness, you are pure consciousness! As I listened intensely to these convincing words which are supported by scientific studies I was flabbergasted to hear Deepak

Chopra not only mention that at subatomic levels our bodies indeed are made up of parts of Jesus, Buddha, a taxi driver in India, trees or animals in the rain forest or any other living or not living being that ever existed.

This was a new concept to me, for the first time ever entered into my consciousness as a result of pure logical deduction, while sitting in the car on my way to this presentation. And now within two hours of having this private revelation I am being presented with knowledge of scientific studies that support this idea.

Should humanity be an experiment of consciousness then today it looks like we could say this experiment has failed. With these words Deepak Chopra continued to explain; we have reached an important crossroad in our existence. On the one hand we can choose to continue living our lives, following the path to self destruction or to find the way to the domain of awareness that exists outside of time. The understanding of this domain is becoming clear to us through quantum physics. Today Science and mathematics are telling us that there is a level of existence in the universe that is non local, where everything is inseparably one. Space, time, information, energy and the material world all dissolves into pure potentiality in this domain which makes it therefore timeless. However, in the spiritual traditions this domain is known as the realm of soul, spirit or consciousness. And as we are part of nature this domain is also part of us.

2.1.4 The EGO has landed.

In the great wisdom traditions of India, time is born when there is a split of consciousness into a subject and an object. As soon as the split occurs in the nervous system, when consciousness differentiates itself in subject and object time is born. Because time is the measurement of experience, the experience measured is always different depending on the location and speed of the observer.

This was explained by Albert Einstein in his relativity theory. Our biological clock which includes the aging process is the metabolism of time. That is why when you're having a good time, time flies, you're bored, time drags, you are running out of time your biological clock speeds up. Everything is in the fast lane, high blood pressure, jittery palates, high levels of adrenaline, faster heart rates and if such a person drops and dies of a heart attack then they have obviously run out of time. So time in many ways is our internal dialogue, it measures how we experience the objects of our perceptions which in fact are part of us, because all objects are experienced in our consciousness and nowhere else.

We were invited to take a journey into the realm of pure potentiality, the place where time does not exist. Just realize that you are surrounded by infinity in every direction, go beyond the observer object split and experience the transcendent domain where there is only timelessness. If you are able to shift your identity from the time bound to the timeless even your biological clock will be influenced. In other words; change your perception of time by resurrecting your soul, which is timeless and your body will be reinvented.

Time is also our internal reference point of measurement when we use our EGO as the basis of all experience. Break the barrier of EGO and you will break the barrier of time.

2.1.5 Misperception of the EGO.

Everywhere I go EGO continues to show up. Why do I choose to allow my EGO such high level of importance, when I understand the restrictions that are imposed on me by doing so?

Life as we know it is time bound and as everything resides within our consciousness so also does time. Therefore consciousness must have some kind of intention with the creation of time. In my view this intention is to take every step of the process of life consciously and learn. Not to learn with the goal of knowing but just to have the experience of learning.

Think about this for a while, everything you become aware of you feel the need to understand. This need to understand automatically pushes you into a process of finding meaning for that of which you have become conscious. At this level it is the awareness of the EGO which is involved in this process and projected back to the sphere of spiritual consciousness.

As the EGO is alive, sent on a mission to survive, learn and with the knowledge; the only way for the EGO to survive is if time continues to exist. Then it is not more than logical that EGO will fight ruthlessly to survive. However, it is the misperception that time resides outside the boundaries of timelessness. This allows the EGO to consider the existence of time to be its only hope for survival (fear of death). You see, by making the EGO conscious of the fact that the time bound is a projection of consciousness that takes place within timelessness then the EGO will know that there is nothing to fear. To survive will become an effortless exercise, because time can never end in timelessness.

I know this can be very confusing, but that is what learning does to us sometimes.

Believe me when I say, I did not imagine this part of bridge to success to be what it has become. I hope however, by spontaneously sharing this experience with you, by giving you a live report on three hours of my life, by offering you the opportunity to have a look into the way my thinking process evolved, you will come to understand who I am and what I am about. And I hope that you will have learned to know me, with all of my shortcomings, to be a traveler on the highway of intention, knowing nothing, trying anything to enjoy the experience of learning. Just like you!

2.1.6 Back and forth.

OK, all of the great minds are saying, in different words the same; we are all interconnected, body, mind, heart and spirit. Consciousness is the source of pure potentiality and through intention we are merely a projection of this consciousness. But what does this mean for those who focus on the process of living, learning and becoming conscious of this experience? Which steps do we take to complete the mission we we're sent out to do, when we entered the domain of the time bound?

Don Blackerby, Ph. D., today, is recognized as the foremost Neuro- Linguistic Programming (NLP) authority on Learning Disabilities, including Attention Deficit Disorder and ADHD. During my quest for knowledge I came across what he calls the *"Logical levels of experience"* which I consider to be the stairway of experience leading us back and forth from the time bound to the timeless.

At the highest level there is the Spiritual or greater system level. One level below is the Identity level followed by the Beliefs and Value level then the Capability Level. At this level Don Blackerby realized that there is a void which needs to be addressed. Below this gap there is the behavior level and finally we come to the lowest level which is the environment level.

To learn is to have an experience and to become conscious by creating meaning to this experience. When you take the first step at the lowest level, you choose the environment you want to be in and the people you choose to have this experience with. You automatically tap into the process of behavior which requires actions to be taken. The question then becomes; which actions must I take to put me in the place I choose to be in? Then follows the question; Am I capable of taking these actions and if not what strategies do I use to invoke proper behavior. Then the belief or values level raises the question; why do I do the things I do, and in response the Identity will confront you with the question who am I? The final step, the spiritual or greater System Level is designed to find meaning in a broader perspective and the question who else do I serve with what I do will become the next focus. Once this final level is reached the process changes direction starting from the top, who else do I serve, going back to where and with whom do I want to be.

This is a simple but effective strategy to guide you through the experience of learning. Especially when used in combination with the previously mentioned emotional freedom technique (EFT).

2.2 Take initiative, control is your responsibility.

It just keeps coming, it's unbelievable. But like I told you at the beginning of this book, everything I need I receive at the moment it is needed, and I am thankful for this. Even while writing *Bridge to Success* it keeps happening, every time I finish a chapter and search for new direction it comes to me through a synchronistic event and instantly I am inspired to write the next chapter. For example this story I am about to share with you started eighteen months ago. It will show you how important it is to take initiative even when you are not sure about what the outcome of your actions will be.

Before I continue with the story, I want to explain that not only the story itself but also the timing by which it surfaced to the foreground and the question, if this is a coincidence, which makes this story relevant to be used in this book.

In fact, as I am writing these words I remember having told this story to someone I met yesterday evening during a reception of one of the foundations where I do voluntary work. It was in reaction to questions asked about my work.

However, today October 4th 2009, it is my youngest daughter, Louise's fourth birthday and we had an early celebration with family and friends. The children are in bed and Mirjam left to celebrate her sister's birthday at her mother's home.

I just finished tidying up the house and I am actually a bit tired. However, before I take a moment to relax I decide to have a look and see if there is mail. Sifting through the e-mail box I, to my surprise, notice a message in my inbox that came to me through my plaxo account. The name of the person that sent the message was a mediation client I had more than eighteen months earlier. I was actually surprised, so I opened my plaxo account and read the message.

The message goes as follow:

"Dear mister Jones,

It is nice to have contact with you through plaxo.

- Without even realizing it I was connected with these clients via plaxo, who for privacy reasons I will call Charles and Mary. - Anyway the message continues;

Mary and I are still happy together, it was a difficult period but we managed to survive the situation. Traveling, motorcycle, photography and everything else god has forbidden, name it we are doing it now. We still travel to China. There is still a small part of the emotional issue that remained, if you know what I mean. But I can distance myself from it better and better every day. I am busy with organizing a photo exposition in Shanghai, for which I received a permit. Coming October 29th Mary and I will be leaving to this wonderful country for which I have developed a passion. On November 2nd the exposition will be opened and I am so much looking forward for this event. I will keep you informed.

Kind regards, Charles."

These are the words of a person I haven't seen or heard of for the last eighteen months. The first time I ever met Mary and Charles was at my Amsterdam office one and a half year earlier. For twenty nine years these people were married, with two children, and their marriage was in serious difficulty. They came to me with the question; can you help us to arrange a divorce that will be as painless as possible for all parties concerned?

I sat them down, we discussed how we were going to work together and once all formalities were taken care of we went right into the session. Each of them was given the opportunity to express what their issue was and after about ten minutes both of them had given their version of the truth I turned to them and said.

I understand that you think that this is the end of your relationship, and I can see that you both have valid reasons for thinking this. However, when I listen to both your stories I cannot help but hear that you have much more reasons for saving this marriage, but you feel the circumstances, over which you believe you do not have any control, are forcing you to break up. For this reason I will ask you to bear with me and be open to what I am going to suggest. My suggestion to you is, before we go into answering the question you came with, we reformulate the question to what is needed for you to once more be happy with each other. After addressing this question we will then go over to answering your first question.

They were surprised to hear this, they gazed at each other for a while and I was glad to hear them accept the challenge. Because of my pledge for confidentiality, I cannot share with you the content of what was discussed. But what I can tell you is that one and a half hour after they accepted the challenge they left my office with some instructions, hand in hand. A month later I called to check how everything was going. I was happy to hear that everything was going well, that was the last contact we had.

This is a perfect example of two people who took the initiative to leave this specific roundabout behind them, even if it meant, each going their own way. However, when confronted with the idea that there might be more possibilities they accepted the challenge and once more took the initiative to find answers to those questions they forgot to ask themselves while caught up, living a life going around in circles.

This is the kind of mediation that gives me satisfaction. Financially it is the worst thing that can happen; to have the situation resolved within one session to an extent that exceeds your client's expectation. This means your work is done, and also your income from this specific case. However, the reward I got from taking part in unlocking the enormous potential that lies hidden in these two people was far more valuable than any financial compensation I could have received. By enabling them to once more love and be loved, to live a life in freedom from the restrictions put upon them by their surroundings and to reconnect with the things they are passionate about, enabling them to create the energy that mostly express who they really are. That is much more valuable than anything I can think of.

Besides the fact that it moved me to take part in this beautiful turn of events and eighteen months later to find out that these two people are still happy, married and enjoying their lives to the fullest in a state of freedom. I want you to know that the universe could not have picked a better moment for me to receive this message from Charles. I was at that specific moment ready to start writing this chapter. The e-mail reminded me that I had this wonderful story stored away in my unconsciousness and instantly I recognized the value of sharing this story with you.

2.2.1 Conviction makes taking initiative easy.

Charles and his wife Mary, by themselves came up with the idea, to search for, find and make an appointment with the mediator. By taking this initiative they started an action to resolve the issues that kept them divided. All of these steps were made without externally being requested to do so. However, their belief system caused them to limit themselves in what possibilities there are and so they expected the outcome of these steps to be a divorce. But once they were presented with other options they had the readiness to embark on a new adventure.

Could you imagine how difficult it must have been for these two people to initiate this process in the first place?

Perhaps the following example is of a complete different category; however, the process is the same. No matter how scary the outcome might seem, this question is being asked every day countless times by billions of people all over the world; do I or do I not initiate this action?

This was also true for Rolihlahla which means, *"To pull a branch of a tree"*, or more colloquially, "troublemaker". On July 18th 1918 when he was born, his parents, Gadla Henry Mphakanyiswa and his third wife Nosekeni Fanny gave him this name, but they could not have imagined how accurate his-story would show them to be when they made this choice. Up until July 2008, he was barred from entering the United States of America – except the United Nations headquarters in Manhattan – without a special waiver from the US Secretary of state, because he was labeled member of a terrorist organization.

Nelson as he was later named in English by his teacher Miss Mdingane lived in a tumultuous country, at a time divided by anything you can think of, was constantly provoked by circumstance. These circumstances forced him to accept the responsibilities that go with being Nelson Mandela.

Even though at that moment he might not have been aware of it, he embarked on changing the course of an entire Nation with the initiatives he took. For example the one in 1948 where he provided free or low cost legal counsel to many blacks who lacked attorney representation or when he committed to non-violent resistance to the apartheid regime and later as leader of the ANC's armed wing started to coordinate sabotage campaigns against military and government targets and making plans for a possible guerrilla war if the sabotage failed to end apartheid. Mandela also took control of raising funds abroad and arranged for paramilitary training of the Spear of the Nation, as the armed militant wing of the ANC was called. Every minute of every day Nelson Mandela was actively taking control of writing history with every decision he made.

He was imprisoned on Robben Island. There he remained for the next eighteen of his twenty-seven years imprisonment. While in jail, his reputation grew and he became widely known as the most significant black leader in South Africa. On the Island the most stringent precautions were made to isolate the political prisoners of which Nelson Mandela was the most known. While in prison Mandela undertook study with the University of London by correspondence through its external program and received the degree of Bachelor of Laws.

An attempt was made to murder him in a fake escape plot that would justify his death. In February 1985 President P.W. Botha offered Mandela conditional release in return for renouncing armed struggle. He declined, releasing a statement via his daughter Zindzi saying "What freedom am I being offered while the organization of the people remains banned? Only free men can negotiate. A prisoner cannot enter into contracts.

Today we know Nelson Mandela to be the first president of South Africa to be elected in a fully representative democratic election.

2.3 Verify that every step you take brings you closer to your goal.

You may have noticed that all steps in the process of creating eventually leads to action. And as you know, every action you take will move you from one place to another. I do not mean only a physical action or move; it can also be a shift in consciousness or any other kind of action or move you can think of. In retrospect very often the question asked is; did I make the right move? However, we often tend to use where we were in the past as our reference point to find the answers to this question.

It is like when you buy a stock on the stock market from a company that is doing well. For a while the stock continues to go up until for no apparent reason it starts to drop. It is a proven fact that very often the investor will find it difficult to sell the stock and take the profit. Even when the stock is at a loss selling becomes more difficult because the original price of the stock and sometimes even the highest value achieved is used as reference point. So the hope that the value of this stock will eventually return to and even beyond the original price will prevent the sale.

In my view this is a mistake, because by looking to the past we turn our back to the future. And if memory serves me right your goals are in front of you and not behind you. So your focus should be towards your goals and not away from them.

If with your last move you did not fully achieve your goal then a fair question would be; how can I get to my goal if I don't know the distance I still have to travel?

I agree with you, you must be aware of your starting point and your finishing point before you can determine what the distance is that you still have to travel to reach your goal. And yes, there are things that must be verified, but instead of analyzing the process of your action it is actually more effective to verify if the results of your action brought you closer to your goal. So in fact what you need to know is where you are at this moment.

I believe that it is more effective to verify where you are at this moment, and if this in fact is where you want to be. Once you've determined that your new starting point is here and now, at the centre of all possible directions, you will notice the sense of freedom that comes with the infinite amount of possibilities to choose from, that stare you in the face from all directions.

You must know how important this is when determining the distance between where you are and where you want to be. Here and now is the starting point from which your next step will be taken. It actually doesn't matter which direction you choose to go however, when you understand better what living in the moment means your choice of direction will automatically bring you closer to the realization of who or what you are intended to be. Because you will understand the principle of letting go of all limiting thoughts that keep you preoccupied with the past.

2.3.1 Living in the moment.

A perfect example of someone who made the decision to live in the moment at a time when all hope was nowhere to be found is author, speaker and spiritual teacher Byron Katie. For her, living in the moment began in 1986; after nearly a decade of struggling with severe depression, alcoholism, suicidal thoughts and eating disorders, she checked herself into a halfway house and rehabilitation centre for women. There it was that Katie had an awakening and became filled with happiness, clarity and calmness that changed her life forever. As she puts it; *'I realized that the cause of my intense suffering and depression was not the world around me, but the beliefs I had about the world.'* This was the turning point in her life; soon she started to share her realization with others and developed a process of self-inquiry called, "The Work." Through The Work, which includes answering and evaluating four key questions, Katie helps people transform their lives and end their suffering by changing their thoughts about themselves and the world around them.

Did you know at this very moment all of your senses are picking up five million impressions simultaneously and sending them at the speed of light through your nervous system? Did you also know that, in search of meaning for these impressions you have between sixty thousand and eighty thousand thoughts per day, and 70% of these thoughts are repeating thoughts? Do you understand that this means; every two seconds you are repeating the same thoughts over and over again.

Now join this with the fact that your constant thoughts become your reality and ask yourself if having the same thoughts every two seconds is constant. In my view it is safe to say yes. If you had the power to choose, which I believe, you do, would you not replace your limiting thoughts with thoughts that will open the doors to all rooms in the palace of possibilities?

You might be thinking, but how is this possible? I am reading this book and I am only aware and thinking of the text that I read, my interpretations thereof, the mood I am in, the room and whatever other things you might be conscious of at this moment. And you are right this is a process that takes place unconsciously.

2.3.2 Why are we blind to the moment?

In one of the most highly cited papers in psychology, The magical number seven, plus or minus two, George Armitage Miller suggested that seven plus or minus two was the magic number that characterizes peoples memory performance on random lists of letters, words, numbers, or almost any kind of meaningful familiar items. This means that our working memory is generally considered to have limited capacity. In other words we are able to process only seven (plus minus two) elements, called chunks, at any given moment. Chunking refers to a strategy to improve efficient use of short term memory by recording and compressing loose items into one collection or unit of information. However, the point is our ability on a conscious level to collect and process information in the moment is very limited. So what happens with the rest of the information we are consciously not able to process?

Today we can only assume that this information goes straight back into that part of consciousness which we are not able to be conscious of. The consciousness where all information resides, each moment of our existence, the same consciousness from which the intention we so desperately struggle to give meaning to was born. Yes, it is the same consciousness that is timeless from which we and everything that exists is a projection of. In our journey of life it is our purpose to restore the unity between the spiritual (consciousness) and the isolated consciousness that resides within us, by adding coherence to our body, mind, heart and spirit. Until coherence is restored we will be limited by the magical number of seven plus minus two. This in fact is the window through which we project the results of our experiences back to our spiritual parents or consciousness.

This is life, the beginning of time, the birth of our ego and the manner in which we are able to have the experience of life. It means taking a journey and in fact going through a process, which takes us every fraction of every second, minute, hour, day, week, month, or year towards what consciousness intended for us to be.

As each process has a beginning and an end, consciousness, which is limitless, cannot in its totality be fitted into this process. So for practical reasons we, the bio body suites we wear, deny the existence of consciousness outside of ourselves and we choose to call it unconsciousness. The funny thing with this trick is, when you give the non existent a name to deny its existence, you actually by default acknowledge its existence.

But how does this information help you to live in the moment?

2.3.3 Benefits of our limitations.

Since by default we acknowledge the existence of consciousness outside ourselves we automatically planted the seed of meaning. This enabled us to work together in search for meaning. For centuries we've built complex societies, cultures, religions, economies, monetary, educational, legal and political systems etc., by use of the meaning we attach to what we have experienced. But still we remain confused and continue the search.

Let's take a look at the world religions, which for centuries held on to the common translation of Genesis 1:1; in the beginning God created heaven and earth. Can you imagine, with the meaning given to this translation, how many millions of people's lives this one sentence, through the years has influenced? For generations societies were built on the assumption that the world was created by God in the beginning. Today, there is evidence that this translation is not correct.

According to Professor Ellen van Wolde, exegesis of the Old Testament at the Radboud University in Nijmegen, this translation is wrong. The mistake lies in one word, *"bara"* which has been translated into creation instead of separation. So in fact the text should be, in the beginning God separated heaven and earth. This implies that the beginning as preached for centuries was not the beginning of creation but of a separation of something else that might have been some kind of unity between heaven and earth.

So what meaning will we give to this new translation to take us from the moment of now into our future? Are we only going to use the meaning of the translation to adapt our actions, or is it also important that we give meaning to the fact that for centuries our actions were based on a creation instead of a separation?

What I can say about this is that it is becoming clear to me that the assumptions we make in the process of building our belief systems are, in due time consistently proven to be false. The world is flat, the heart is in our head, one race is superior to the other, in the beginning the world was created etc. However, we humans have been able to create everything that we are at this moment conscious of, successfully, by use of these belief systems. When I say successful I do this with disregard to the following questions. Is everyone happy with the outcome of what we've created or wether these belief systems are correct or not. I'm not talking about the results, what I mean is the process of creation itself is a success. Today, by use of our belief systems, we have successfully transformed energy into the manifestation of this world we live in.

Understand; this was done from the perspective of our limitations. We are continuously creating the future from the perspective of the past including all the limitations we imposed upon ourselves; in other words we are standing with our faces directed at the past trying to create the future. This is how we, without knowing, allow ourselves to be led by our shadows as the light of the future is shining behind us instead of ahaid of us.

So imagine what possibilities lie ahead of us when we take this moment as the starting point to harness the true and pure energy that flows through our hearts, minds, bodies and souls and decide to jointly build a world filled with enough positive energy to leave behind us the lights of the past that we so desperately fight to keep shining.

2.4 Use the energy you create as your compass.

Time is a finite resource and therefore, when we choose to subject our reality to time we automatically limit ourselves to the restrictions imposed on us by time. That is exactly what we have been doing for centuries. Where we are today is a direct result of this behavior. Now the question is; are we happy with the results? If not, then would it be desirable to replace the resource that causes limitations with one that is limitless? The answer to this question in my view is absolutely yes!

So, what resources do we have at our disposal that fits the job description? I believe this resource to be energy. In physics energy is defined as the amount of work that can be performed by a force, an attribute of objects and systems that is subject to a conservation law. But of course this definition was also subject to limitations. Anyway, it is my view that our body, emotion, mind and spirit, acts as a transformer to cause the energy that comes from consciousness to be transformed into action or as the definition states, work.

When you realize that energy you use to maintain an idea, emotion or belief, which in fact means to continually repeat the same action, this energy will be occupied and not available for any other use. Simply put; unless your hands are free, you cannot accept what's given to you without first paying attention to that which you are already carrying. The moment will then be lost to the past.

So when you step into the moment of now, make sure your hands are free and you are ready and able to catch whatever falls from the sky or to pick up what lies at your feet without first being distracted by the questions; what must I let go of first and what does letting go mean for my future?

This is how you keep your antennea or reticular formation fine tuned to receive and understand information coming from consciousness that is meant for you. Once you decide to pay full attention to hear, see, feel, know and let go of all preconditioned responses and expectations you will be amazed by the enormous possibilities that are presented to you every moment.

2.4.1 Energy versus time.

Tony Schwartz wrote a piece for the pages of Harvard Business Review about increasing your energy capacity is the best way to get more work done faster and better. Schwartz and his colleagues at the energy project advocate that by establishing specific rituals, - behaviors that are intentionally practiced and precisely scheduled with the goal of making them unconscious and automatic as quickly as possible - we can systematically expand and renew the energy levels in each of the four main energy dimensions; the body, emotions, mind and spirit.

The body: Physical energy.

Inadequate nutrition, -exercise, -sleep and rest diminish people's basic energy levels as well as their ability to manage their emotions and focus their attention.

The emotions: Quality of energy.

When people are able to take control of their emotions they can improve the quality of their energy regardless of the external pressures they are facing. To do this they first must become aware of how they feel at various points during the work day and of the impact these emotions have on their effectiveness. Most people realize that they tend to perform best when they are feeling positive energy. What they find surprising is that they are not able to perform well or to lead effectively when they are feeling any other way.

The mind: Focus of energy.

Many executives view multi-tasking as a necessity in the face of all the demands they juggle. But it actually undermines productivity, distractions are costly, a temporary shift in attention from one task to another, stopping to answer an e-mail or to take a phone call for instance, increases the amount of time necessary to finish the primary task by as much as twenty five percent. A phenomenon known as switching time, it's far more efficient to fully focus for ninety to one hundred and twenty minutes. Take a true break and then fully focus on the next activity.

The human spirit: Energy of meaning and purpose.

People tap into the energy of the human spirit when their every day work and activities are consistent with what they value most, and with what gives them a sense of meaning and purpose. If the work they are doing really matters to them they typically feel more positive energy, focus better and demonstrate greater perseverance.

In his study Tony Schwartz and his colleagues, at the energy project focused first on the physical energy, they searched for excessive energy depleting activities then established specific rituals to replace them with. Then they repeated this process for each of the energy levels; body, emotions, mind and spirit. They found that many people don't even recognize meaning or purpose as potential sources of energy. To prevent confusion they choose to start the program with physical energy, which generally is accepted to be an energy source and follow through towards energy of meaning and purpose.

However, this study shows that there is much to be gained when we make the shift from using the limitations that time imposes on us, as the foundation on which we shape our lives to instead explore and use the infinite potentials that energy possesses, but is hidden from us because of our ignorance. To do this we must turn our antennea on and tune into the spiritual frequency through which consciousness is transmitting its intention to us. Once we are aware of these intentions, the way we use our body, emotions, mind and spirit to channel energy through our actions, will change and what we are intended to be will automatically become of us.

More than two thousand years ago the great Greek philosophers, Socrates and Aristotle in their studies of normative ethics or moral theory came up with similar ideas about this topic. Even though the wording is different, in essence what they say supports to a great extent the conclusion of most of today's gurus. So for more than two thousand years we are struggling with the same questions and coming up with the same answers. However, we cannot seem to find the way to apply them. To achieve happiness and success we must focus our attention on the core of who we are, learn to understand what we are intended to be and just be.

To illustrate this, I will share with you the idea's of these two Greek philosophers:

Socrates
Socrates was one of the first to encourage scholars and common citizen to turn their attention from the outside world to the condition of man. In his view self-knowledge is considered necessary for success and inherently an essential good. A self-aware person will act completely within his/her capabilities to their pinnacle, while an ignorant person will flounder and encounter difficulty. To Socrates, a person must become aware of every fact (and its context) relevant to his existence, if he wishes to attain self-knowledge. The assumption was that people will naturally do what is good, if they know what is right. Evil or bad actions are the result of ignorance. If a criminal were truly

aware of the mental and spiritual consequences of his actions, he would neither commit nor even consider committing those actions. Any person who knows what is truly right will automatically do it, according to Socrates. While he correlated knowledge with virtue, he similarly equated virtue with happiness. The truly wise man will know what is right, do what is good, and therefore be happy.

Aristotle
Aristotle posited an ethical system that may be termed "self- realisationism." In Aristotle's view, when a person acts in accordance with his nature and realizes his full potential, he will do well and be content. At birth, a baby is not a person, but a potential person. In order to become a "real" person, the child's inherent potential must be realized. Unhappiness and frustration are caused by the unrealized potential of a person, leading to failed goals and a poor life. Aristotle said, "Nature does nothing in vain." Therefore, it is imperative for persons to act in accordance with their nature and develop their latent talents, in order to be content and complete. Happiness was held to be the ultimate goal. All other things, such as civic life or wealth, are merely means to the end. Self-realization, the awareness of one's nature and

the development of one's talents, is the surest path to happiness.

Aristotle asserted that man had three natures: vegetable (physical), animal (emotional) and rational (mental). Physical nature can be assuaged through exercise and care, emotional nature through indulgence of instinct and urges and mental through human reason and developed potential. Rational development was considered the most important, as essential to philosophical self-awareness and as uniquely human. Moderation was encouraged, with the extremes seen as degraded and immoral. For example, courage is the moderate virtue between the extremes of cowardice and recklessness. Man should not simply live, but live well with conduct governed by moderate virtue. This is regarded as difficult, as virtue denotes doing the right thing, to the right person, at the right time, to the proper extent, in the correct fashion, for the right reason.

Take a closer look at the difficulty of virtue in Aristotle's meaning of the word and you will see that it comes down to finding answers for these six important questions; what..., who..., when..., how much..., how... and why....

Is it coincidence that the most questions ever asked in the past and still today by people all over the world are focused on finding the answer to; what..., who..., when..., how much..., how... and why...?

So you see it took us at least two thousand years to find the right questions. However, unfortunately we too often ask them judgmentally of others and all together forget to ask them with care of ourselves.

2.4.2 Building bridges.

Now we have reached the point where we can start building the bridge to your success. We have all the tools needed and we know how to use them. In fact, you actually already made the first step to build the bridge when you decided to think different thoughts. Since you've gotten this far with reading *Bridge to Success* I can safely assume that you now understand that if your constant thoughts become your truth and reality then your next conclusion will be that your reality of today was created by the thoughts you had yesterday. And, the thoughts you have today will become tomorrow's reality. But how do you find new thoughts every day and are you able to process them within the limitations of time?

First let me remind you: in chapter one you already learned how to create by use of your imagination. And this is exactly the same process you will use to create new thoughts.

Secondly I once more want to bring to your attention that every day up to eighty thousand thoughts goes through your mind. Seventy percent are repetition, which means up to fifty six thousand old thoughts are being repeated endlessly. What would happen to your thinking capacity if you could let go of ten, twenty or maybe even fifty percent of the fifty six thousand repetitions? Will this not make room for that many new thoughts and increase your thinking capacity by one new thought every ten, five or two seconds? This means you will be able to process between five thousand six hundred and twenty eight thousand additional new thoughts per day.

This suggests that by holding on to old thoughts you use up energy that can otherwise be used for new or different thoughts.

It is like a computer: in the morning when you turn it on and start up Microsoft Word to type a letter, the system is working perfect at top speed. As the day progresses you work with outlook, excel, explorer, and other applications. But you never bother to close these applications after use. However, its noon and the computer's response time starts to increase. At the end of the day you notice that the letter you typed in the morning was not saved and you must retype this exact same letter. However, while typing you notice the computer is working slowly and you begin to feel irritated. Eventually it takes you more than twice the time it took in the morning to re-type the same letter. You see, even though the applications you started up during the day are not actively being used, they occupy space and continue to use energy as long as you don't close them.

This means, the energy being used at the end of the day is much more than in the morning, even though consciously you are doing the exact same work.

But what you must realize is that even though the applications are not being used the computer is constantly repeating its routine to save and refresh the settings of these programs and therefore, the capability of the system to type your letter is much less than it was in the morning.

So, to make the mind shift, and let go of old recurring thoughts, you must complete tasks, which in my computer analogy I equate with closing all applications after use. This will prevent you from having old thoughts repeated over and over again.

2.4.3 CARE in a nutshell; part two.

The CARE System is a consistent process aimed at instantly finding where you are in life, knowing where you want to be, getting you there and ultimately knowing and being you on all levels.

In part one I discussed the concept of IDEA, which created the bridge between what consciousness intended us to be, and what we choose to believe, or presume to be our intention.

That part of the process, which is 80% an internal process, is too often taken for granted. Consciously we do not care much about this part and allow ourselves to react to situations routinely. We do not, in full awareness, benefit from these tools, and we even forget we possess the tools to start building the bridges to our success. By really putting CARE and thus 100% of your attention into this process you will at all times be aware of where you are and keep focus on where you want to be.

Part two is where IDEA is externalized and to some degree materializes by way of word of mouth, writings and actions. This is where we apply or LIVE our IDEA. This stands for: Learn, to take Initiative, Verify the effects of your expressions and to create the Energy that represents who you are. The concept of LIVE is actually to apply your IDEA in an external process, where the interaction between you and your surroundings will alter your belief and eventually shape what you intended to create, through your respective expectations. This process is shown in the following figure;

Fig 2.

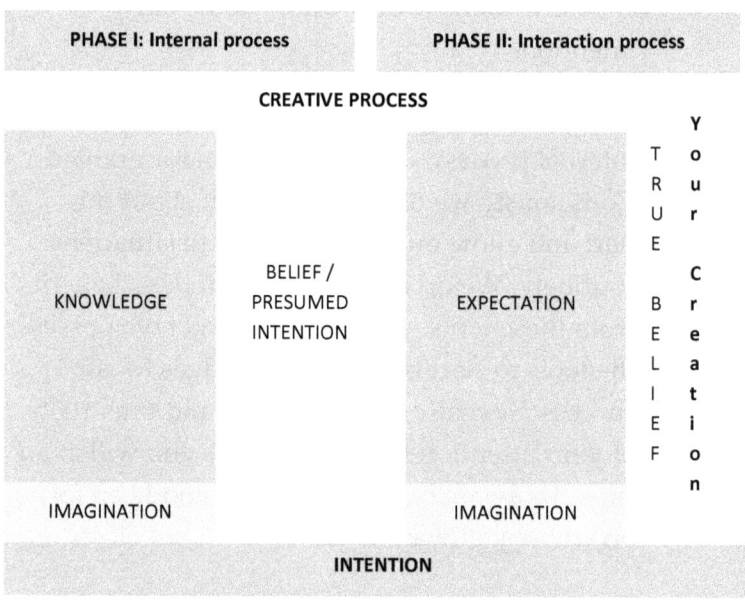

Intention still lies at the foundation of everything ever created or yet to be created and continues to act as the highway throughout all possible stages of existence ultimately leading to goals.

PHASE II

You will notice that the CARE system is on all levels an interactive process. You will notice that issues discussed in one part will be re-activated in other parts. Like the concept of IDEA which is discussed in part one, LIVE is discussed in part two or Expectation, also discussed in part one but also playing an active role in part two.

Once your belief or presumed intention is externalized, your surroundings will expect something of you and the interaction caused will lead you to expect something in return. These expectations which in fact are merely consistent thoughts will eventually become your belief, your truth, and your reality.

Again you have the option to use your imagination to uncover mis-interpretations or false links which can lead you to hold on to beliefs, even though they limit you in achieving your goals.

Instead of caring more for learning, taking initiative, verifying that every step you take is one taking you closer to your goal and ultimately using the energy you create as your compass, you choose to put more attention and care into what your expectations are or what is expected of you. This is a classic mistake most of us so often make.

We let go of the experience of living and hold on to finding meaning and justification for our expectations. We allow ourselves to be caught up in the everlasting loop between belief/presumed intention – expectation – true belief and the energy we create.

This is the second phase of your internal conflict. Eventually you will once more come to a compromise and allow your presumed intention to become your true belief and everything you create will have this true belief as its foundation.

To avoid going around in circles following daily, weekly, monthly and yearly patterns that every so often repeats itself, you must become conscious of, and learn how to use the many tools you have at your disposal. One of the most important tools is your imagination. Yes, also in this phase Imagination is an important tool which you can use to break the cycle that holds you captive in your limiting beliefs.

The process of creation is a constant process, going back and forth. All phases are interconnected, held together by consciousness's consistent and patient whispers of its intentions to you, every step of the way. It is up to you to listen, to feel, to smell, to see and to understand what you need to do to make the right things happen.

As long as you, like most people, continue to care more for the loud noises that comes with the inner conflicts and miss the silent whispers leading to your goals you, like 80% of all humans, in more than 80% of the time, will remain in search of confirmation.

3 Reflect

The higher self is that place where everything is accomplished. A mere desire becomes the trigger for transformation.

-Deepak Chopra-

In psychology self-reflection is called introspection which is a process of self-observation and reporting of conscious inner thoughts, desires and sensations. Which in essence is the way our nervous system, on a conscious level, transforms raw information through thoughts and emotions into specific actions. Important in this process is the use of thinking, reasoning and examining of your own thoughts, feelings and on a spiritual level, your soul. This process is aimed at understanding the conflicts of the human heart, mind or body and the effect this has on behavior.

3.1 Examine the effect of your idea.

Our behavior, or the actions we undertake have an effect on ourselves, other people, the environment we live in and how others perceive us. Through contemplation or self-observation we try to assess the effects of our conscious inner thoughts, desires and sensations.

However, even though most of the time we are not aware of them there are also thoughts, desires and sensations we experience on an unconscious level. To apply the CARE system effectively you must get in contact with these unconscious issues you somehow managed to suppress to the extent that you are no more aware of their existence and don't even understand how they have an effect on your day to day life.

Every day all over the world thousands of professionals like doctors, psychologists, psychiatrists, mental coaches, motivational speakers and others spend time trying to unravel this mystery in an attempt to help us find new direction, energy and drive to continue our travel along life's highway.

As you may understand, with this part of the process some external help can be useful. This is not because there is something wrong with you, but because it is sometimes easier for someone else to help you recognize your unconscious patterns.

In fact we often receive help from friends and family while they tell us what they see, hear and feel, and the effects our behavior has on them. But we often refuse to understand and sometimes even push them away.

This is why in many cases a professional coach, psychologist or motiovatinal speaker can be useful.

Previously I mentioned briefly Byron Katie's *"The Work"*, Richard Bandler and John Grinder's *"NLP"* and Gary Craig's *"EFT"* emotional freedom techniques.

These are all techniques that each on their own has proven to be effective. However, I frequently use a combination of these three techniques during my coaching and counseling sessions. And the rewards for my cliënts have proven to be great.

Suppressed issues lay at the core of negative emotions. And these emotions cause the body's electrical or nervous system to be disrupted, as if there is a short circuit. During the course of our lives when these emotions are triggered we tend to lose control of our behavior.

To restore the balance in the disruptive electrical or nervous system I often use EFT. This technique has proven to be a simple and effective tool to deal with these issues and any one can learn to use EFT on themselves.

In addition I use a combination of *"The Work"*, *"NLP"*, *"Intuition"* and *"Common Sense"* to uncover the core issues to be treated.

In the following chapter I will discuss examples of suppressed issues which I call X-Factor.

3.2 X-Factor, gifts we receive but cannot unwrap.

I've seen and heard of many examples that illustrate how, when you take initiative, are in control and accept responsibility for your actions, you will become conscious of every phrase written in every chapter of your history. You must be aware, that even as you read these words, you are involved in the process of writing your own history. Your personal history and the history you share with others during your life.

The process of writing history is in fact a process where electrical impulses in your nervous system are processed; connections are being made between your interpretations of your memories, which become your thoughts and your emotions.

These connections become impulses for you to act upon. This means that the actions you choose to take are actions taken as a direct result of your interpretations of your memories and you are therefore actually writing your history based on combinations and connections between these memories, thoughts and emotions. But what if, for whichever reason, these connections are screwed up and mistakes were made. Remember this is a process taking place unconsciously and therefore you are not aware of these mistakes. And there is no way you could find out until you take the time to reflect on the effects of your actions on you and your surroundings.

What will happen to you and the reality you've created about yourself, the people around you and the way you've lived your life for so many years? What will you do, who will you become when you are aware of these bad connections that causes anxiety, confusion, emotional discomfort, physical ailments, mental and other ailments. Wouldn't you want to know how to correct these bad connections which I call X-factors?

3.2.1 My father's prison walls.

This reminds me of my promise to tell you what happened to me on an emotional level the day I found myself in the ditch. I will combine this with another story to show how these X-Factors are created, what effect they have and how they can be passed on from one person to another.

As a child I had an open personality, spontaneous, curious, and witty and always looking for things to undertake. Learning and understanding new and different things was and still is my passion. I remember one Christmas Season in an attempt to get the children interested in doing more chores around the house my mom came up with the idea of a competition.

My parents did not have much money to buy presents for all ten of the children. One gift was bought; a brand new Timex watch and we all had to compete to win this prize.

The child that did the most chores and behaved the best in the period from the beginning of December to the 24th would win this watch. When I received my prize on Christmas day I was happy.

I treasured it intensely; however, my curiosity grew by the day to find out what makes this watch tick. A few months later I found myself in a state of timelessness trying to satisfy my curiosity by taking the watch apart. Two days had gone by as if not more than five minutes had passed. At the end of the second day I realized that the watch was, to the smallest part, dismantled and put back together. Fortunately it still kept the correct time.

I could spend days, weeks and even months taking things apart and putting them back together. Sometimes they functioned better after the operation and sometimes worse. But that did not stop me from taking the television, radio or washing machine apart, which often got me into trouble.

Despite the poverty my life as a child was rich. I enjoyed the freedom that came with living on a small island where it seemed that everyone knew each other. And raising kids was not only the task of the parents, but of the whole community. Besides, my brothers, sisters and I were guaranteed safety by the fame my dad had as "The bruiser". Everyone was afraid of his directness and his ability to punch out even the largest of men who challenged him to a fight or even those, who in his mind said the wrong thing at the wrong time. My dad was hit first ask questions later. This way of being most probably came from his continued struggle to survive which he developed during his childhood as an orphan.

My dad never met his father and his mother died when he was five years old. From that moment he had to fend for himself. He had an aunt, who due to pressure from the community accepted him to stay with her family. But the brutality of an everyday beating and other hardships inflicted on him suggests that not having this aunt might have been better for his personal development. However, the circumstances dictated to him; you must learn to fight to defend yourself if you want to survive. And indeed my father's whole life has been fighting.

Even yesterday during Louise's birthday while I spoke with my dad I noticed the constant struggle he is waging. It hurts when I look into my father's eyes and see the pain he never talks about, the rage that he still, to some extent, managed to contain and the beauty inside he actually never found a way to express. Except for the rare moments when he let his guard down. In all of my father's actions, the way he speaks and the intensity with which he reacts to situations, it is clear to see that he is lashing out at all the wrong done to him from the moment his mother died, and his inability to channel the built up negative energy that holds him imprisoned.

I believe that he was not even conscious of the effect his behavior had on his surroundings. For him it was pure survival. And my father in fact became a master at building walls. Walls behind which he kept hidden the true emotional meaning he gave to the events that caused him so much pain as a child.

I believe this to be true to the extent that he is now suffering from Alzheimer disease. His constant struggle to suppress his emotions has become such a fundamental part of his being. And now the only logical result is becoming evident by way of the suppression of all of his memory, rather than dealing with the emotions.

3.2.2 How my father's prison walls became mine.

Remember, your constant thoughts become your reality, and so my father's constant thoughts were; fight to survive and suppress the memories of events that cause pain and sadness. I believe, my father as a child took a vow. What this vow was I do not know but what I do know is that the events leading up to the moment he took the vow kept him totally and completely focused on only one thing and that is to survive and to forget.

However, the survival techniques he thought himself as a kid took a hold of him. It prevented him from realizing that he had a wonderful wife, who is willing and able to support him in his struggle, seven sons and four daughters who for a great part of their lives silently hoped to see their father's true nature.

However, as I previously discussed, humans tend to learn by example and as my father was a proficient master at building walls to hide the painful scars and emotions, I had no other option than to spontaneously use these traits bestowed upon me on an unconscious level by my father.

While standing in that ditch, I realized the pain that can be caused by just a few words from a stranger, it also became clear to me how vulnerable I was in this new world full of strangers. I never knew I was that proficient in building walls. Instantaneously my walls were reaching for the sky. Without one moment's hesitation my mind was made up. My vow was ready to put into practice; no one else but me is going to decide who gets a view of the inside of my walls.

For a long time I lived my life behind these walls only letting in what I believed to be safe. Any one that in any way could cause me pain was radically excommunicated. But I was lucky to also have my mom as an example. Even though it was from behind my walls, I was able to always show kindness, care for and be helpful to people, even though I refused to let anyone come too close. This modus operandi was a direct result of this one event in my life. It caused me to hide my true self from the world. The child I once was became only known to me.

By accepting a stranger to dictate what is written in this chapter of my history I tried to escape from taking responsibility, which in my view is the same as rejecting a part of me. And as I firmly believe that you must become one with yourself before you can enjoy the experience of success, it is out of the question for me not to accept responsibility for all of my thoughts, emotions, and behavior because ultimately it is no one else but me who will be held accountable for my actions. This is why I must be fully in charge.

3.3 People.

My eight year old son, Kiran, not sure of how to approach me teamed up with his mother to remind me of my promise to him. One day at school he told his friend, Jan, that he would build his own waveboard.

After school he told me this story and I asked him; what was Jan's response. "Jan laughed at me and said this is impossible; you can't build a waveboard." Kiran continued by saying,"but I told Jan, you are so foolish, didn't you know; everything is possible!" After sharing this information with me Kiran asked if I could help him build his new waveboard. And of course, even though I had never seen or heard of a waveboard before, I said yes.

Now, two weeks later his patience was running out and it was time to collect on this promise. The message is not only to fulfill this promise but also to remind me that it is my duty to practice what I preach. As the words he used to convince his friend; 'everything is possible', came from my mouth.

But what is more interesting about this situation is that my son in fact was telling me; dad there is still some work to be done on breaking down your walls. He was actually inviting me to remember; to revisit my childhood where I intensely enjoyed those moments where time did not exist. A period in my life where my day dreams seemed to be my everyday reality and also the time when I made a vow to help at least five million people before I die.

3.3.1 The art of giving and receiving.

Why would a twelve year old child, who is living in a consistent dream, make such a vow? Does this say anything about the interpretation I had about my spiritual intentions? And if it does, what was this interpretation? At this moment I don't know what it meant, however, at twelve, without knowing how to achieve this, I made a firm decision to give something positive to at least five million people with the intention of helping them in one way or another.

As far as I know, my intention at that moment was to give for the sake of giving without expecting anything in return. It was as if I recognized a need and spontaneously volunteered to fill it. But still, in retrospect what I've received in return, over the years, is amazing to me and I am grateful for the opportunity to have received the life that led me towards living my dreams today.

I live a happy life by simply giving happiness to the people around me and wishing it for others I see struggling to find it. I live a life full of love by simply giving my love to people I am in contact with and sending it to those at a distance. I enjoy friendships, joy and abundance by simply giving it to the people around me and trying to inspire them to tap into the vast potentials hidden inside of them to find the friendships that suits them best and to attract abundance in ways they never thought possible.

For as far back in time as I could remember, I've lived my life using these laws bestowed upon me by my mother. It wasn't until I became an adult I realized these laws where the laws of giving and receiving. And once I had gathered enough courage to face the greatest challenge of taming my mind, in search of the silent moments of timelessness I experienced so often as a child, I started to hear a whisper. It was the same whisper I used to wake up to as a child. This word, "Love" for some time now is frequently whispered into my ears, and once again it becomes my consistent thought.

With the knowledge I now have, that humans are shaped by their thoughts and we become what we think, I know, now it is my duty to take great care and guard this thought that is subtle, difficult to perceive and slips out of reach at the tiniest opportunity. I am convinced that once I am fully tuned into the frequency on which this constant whisper is spoken, I will eventually hear and understand the total message. And even though I am a far way from helping five million people, I will, before I die, fulfill this promise my twelve year old self made. And I will understand that even though, to me it seems to be an enormous task, in the grand scheme of things, this deed is merely a tiny sprinkle in the vast ocean of love. However, it is my responsibility to, in one way or another, make a positive difference in the lives of at least five million people.

3.4 Love = E=MC² = Consciousness.

Intuitively we consider love to be something good. But when asked what love is, either a million different answers will be given or none. And both reactions are correct as there isn't one conclusive definition of what love is. About love, Lao Tzu said; 'the name that can be named is not the eternal name. The unnamable is the eternally real. If you focus on the name, you lose the substance. So, can love be defined? No, if we live it. And yes, for all other purposes.'

3.4.1 The source of the writings on our walls.

Love is proven to be something beyond ones' grasp. We lose the essence of love when we focus on trying to understand the meaning instead of living out its purpose. In the next section I will take you through the world of religions, and how, according to these predominant religions, love should be experienced.

It is strange to see that even though there is to some degree consensus on the origin of love, still, throughout history, 100% of all major wars in the world find its origin in the different interpretations of fundamental issues such as what does love mean. Perhaps this is the result of the fact that for centuries we have allowed the world religions to write on our walls in the name of love. It is as if we interpret religion to be the source of love. Let's take a look at what these religions say about love.

Judaism
Source: Wikipedia

In Hebrew, Ahava is the most commonly used term for both interpersonal love and love of God. Judaism employs a wide definition of love, both among people and between man and the Deity. Regarding the former, the Torah states, "Love your neighbor like yourself" (Leviticus 19:18). As for the latter, one is commanded to love God "with all your heart, with all your soul and with all your might" (Deuteronomy 6:5), taken by the Mishnah (a central text of the Jewish oral law) to refer to good deeds, willingness to sacrifice one's life rather than commit certain serious transgressions, willingness to sacrifice all of one's possessions, and being grateful to the Lord despite adversity (tractate Berachoth 9:5). Rabbinic literature differs as to how this love can be developed, e.g., by contemplating divine deeds or witnessing the marvels of nature. As for love between marital partners, this is deemed an essential ingredient to life: "See life with the wife you love" (Ecclesiastes 9:9). The biblical book Song of

Solomon is considered a romantically phrased metaphor of love between God and his people, but in its plain reading, reads like a love song. The 20th-century Rabbi Eliyahu Eliezer Dessler is frequently quoted as defining love from the Jewish point of view as "giving without expecting to take" (from his Michtav me-Eliyahu, Vol. 1).

Christianity
Source: Wikipedia
Sacred Love versus Profane Love (1602–03) by Giovanni Baglione

The Christian understanding is that love comes from God. The love of man and woman — Eros in Greek — and the unselfish love of others (agape), are often contrasted as "ascending" and "descending" love, respectively, but are ultimately the same thing.

There are several Greek words for "love" that are regularly referred to in Christian circles.

Agape: In the New Testament, agapē is charitable, selfless, altruistic, and unconditional. It is parental love, seen as creating goodness in the world; it is the way God is seen to love humanity, and it is seen as the kind of love that Christians aspire to have for one another.

Phileo: Also used in the New Testament, phileo is a human response to something that is found to be delightful, also known as "brotherly love."

Two other words for love in the Greek language, eros (sexual love) and storge (child-to-parent love), were never used in the New Testament.

Christians believe that to Love God with all your heart, mind, and strength and Love your neighbor as yourself are the two most important things in life (the greatest commandment of the Jewish Torah, according to Jesus; cf. Gospel of Mark chapter 12, verses 28–34). Saint Augustine summarized this when he wrote "Love God, and do as thou wilt."

The Apostle Paul glorified love as the most important virtue of all. Describing love in the famous poem in 1 Corinthians, he wrote, "Love is patient, love is kind. It does not envy, it does not boast, it is not proud. It is not rude, it is not self-seeking, it is not easily angered, and it keeps no record of wrongs. Love does not delight in evil but rejoices with the truth. It always protects, always trusts, always hopes, and always perseveres." (1 Cor. 13:4–7, NIV)

The Apostle John wrote, "For God so loved the world that he gave his one and only Son, that whoever believes in him shall not perish but have eternal life. For God did not send his Son into the world to condemn the world, but to save the world through him. Whoever believes in him is not condemned, but whoever does not believe stands condemned already because he has not believed in the name of God's one and only Son." (John 3:16–18, NIV)

John also wrote, "Dear friends, let us love one another for love comes from God. Everyone who loves has been born of God and knows God. Whoever does not love does not know God, because God is love." (1 John 4:7–8, NIV)

Saint Augustine says that one must be able to decipher the difference between love and lust. Lust, according to Saint Augustine, is an over indulgence, but to love and be loved is what he has sought for his entire life. He even says, "I was in love with love." Finally, he does fall in love and is loved back, by God. Saint Augustine says the only one who can love you truly and fully is God, because love with a human only allows for flaws such as "jealousy, suspicion, fear, anger, and contention." According to Saint Augustine, to love God is "to attain the peace which is yours." (Saint Augustine's Confessions) Christian theologians see God as the source of love, which is mirrored in humans and their own loving relationships. Influential Christian theologian C.S. Lewis wrote a book called The Four Loves.

Benedict XVI wrote his first encyclical on "God is love." He said that a human being, created in the image of God, who is love, is able to practice love; to give himself to God and others (agape) and by receiving and experiencing God's love in contemplation (eros). This life of love, according to him, is the life of the saints such as Teresa of Calcutta and the Blessed Virgin Mary and is the direction Christians take when they believe that God loves them.

Islam and Arab religions
Source: Wikipedia

In a sense, love does encompass the Islamic view of life as universal brotherhood that applies to all who hold the faith. There are no direct references stating that God is love, but amongst the 99 names of God (Allah), there is the name Al-Wadud, or "the Loving One," which is found in Surah 11:90 as well as Surah 85:14. It refers to God as being "full of loving kindness." All who hold the faith have God's love, but to what degree or effort he has pleased God depends on the individual itself.

Ishq, or divine love, is the emphasis of Sufism. Sufis believe that love is a projection of the essence of God to the universe. God desires to recognize beauty, and as if one looks at a mirror to see oneself, God "looks" at itself within the dynamics of nature. Since everything is a reflection of God, the school of Sufism practices to see the beauty inside the apparently ugly. Sufism is often referred to as the religion of love. God in Sufism is referred to in three main terms, which are the Lover, Loved, and Beloved, with the last of these terms being often seen in Sufi poetry. A common viewpoint of Sufism is that through love, humankind can get back to its inherent purity and grace. The saints of Sufism are infamous for being "drunk" due to their love of God; hence, the constant reference to wine in Sufi poetry and music.

Eastern religions Buddhism
Source: Wikipedia

In Buddhism, Kāma is sensuous, sexual love. It is an obstacle on the path to enlightenment, since it is selfish. Karuā is compassion and mercy, which reduces the suffering of others. It is complementary to wisdom and is necessary for enlightenment. Advea and mettā are benevolent love. This love is unconditional and requires considerable self-acceptance. This is quite different from ordinary love, which is usually about attachment and sex and which rarely occurs without self-interest. Instead, in Buddhism it refers to detachment and unselfish interest in others' welfare.

The Bodhisattva ideal in Mahayana Buddhism involves the complete renunciation of oneself in order to take on the burden of a suffering world. The strongest motivation one has in order to take the path of the Bodhisattva is the idea of salvation within unselfish, altruistic love for all sentient beings.

Hinduism
Source: Wikipedia

In Hinduism, Kāma is pleasurable, sexual love, personified by the god Kamadeva. For many Hindu schools, it is the third end (artha) in life. Kamadeva is often pictured holding a bow of sugar cane and an arrow of flowers; he may ride upon a great parrot. He is usually accompanied by his consort Rati and his companion Vasanta, lord of the spring season. Stone images of Kaama and Rati can be seen on the door of the Chenna Keshava temple at Belur in Karnataka in India. Maara is another name for Kāma.

In contrast to Kāma, prema – or prem – refers to elevated love. Karuna is compassion and mercy, which impels one to help reduce the suffering of others. Bhakti is a Sanskrit term, meaning "loving devotion to the supreme God." A person who practices bhakti is called a bhakta. Hindu writers, theologians, and philosophers have distinguished nine forms of bhakti, which can be found in the Bhagavata Purana and works by Tulsidas. The philosophical work Narada Bhakti Sutras, written by an unknown author (presumed to be Narada), distinguishes eleven forms of love.

3.4.2 How to vibrate love.

It is my firm belief that like consciousness itself, love is pure, as love comes from consciousness. Whether you call it God, Allah, Jehovah, Kamadeva or any other name, consciousness, through intention is confronting us with the experience of love. However, it is often the meaning we choose to give to love that makes us want to have it. So we, for a great part of our lives, go in search of love in all places you can think of. We often expect it to be given to us, we use the idea of love as a bargaining chip and sometimes we even demand it from others.

What we must realize is that the spark of light, at the centre of the diamond that you are, is the bearer of the pure love you seek outside yourself. Learn how to ignite that spark of light within you, by simply giving love, without expecting anything in return. The love will automatically be vibrated back and forth through you. You will be overwhelmed with love.

This experience will give you a sense of expanding outward. The beginning of the creation of something much larger than you; on this level of life you will effortlessly step outside the boundaries of your comfort zone and explore possibilities of connecting with all that lives.

The following exercise is designed to reach within you to vibrate the love you have inside and to send it out towards someone or a group of people you care to share your love with. The exercise is a modern version of some ancient meditations. It has no particular affiliation to any of the religions or New Age teachings. It can be used by anyone, causing no conflict with faith/religions or beliefs. Try it and see what happens, it takes only a few minutes.
1. Find a quite place you know you will not be disturbed. Sit down where you are

comfortable. Let your arms be loose by your side. Take a few deep breaths straight down till under your belly button, breathe fully in and exhale. Repeat a few times until you feel completely relaxed.

2. Now, imagine a person you wish to send love to. It is possible to imagine the whole world or all of humanity. However, start by making it personal. As you breathe in imagine that person into your chest. Hold your breath for a while and just allow your love for that person to fill your chest. The goal is to take him or her into your heart, and love him or her deeply.

3. As you breathe out, send out all the love you can feel from your heart and soul. Take your time, don't hurry the breath, but don't slow it down either, let it just be. If you want to, imagine a warm glow or light surrounding this person as you send your love. Remember, sending or giving love is about the other person and not about you or what you expect they can give or do for you.

4. Close your eyes and pause for a second. Rest within yourself, see what happens. Repeat the process of breathing in that person and breathing him or her out. As you inhale breathe

him/her into your heart, as you exhale send them love.

5. Once you learn to send love without expecting anything in return, then you can start receiving it. As you breathe in, feel yourself receiving love, being filled with it, surrounded by it, bathed in it, healed by it, moved by it and empowered by it. Don't try to think about it, just feel it.

6. You can also add a physical dimension to the receiving of love. As you breathe in let your chest rise and open your fists and feel love coming to you, and you receiving it.

Sometimes as you send out love you'll feel your chest detach itself from your body and something powerful leaving your heart and body. Other times, you will feel love leave your heart and then come right back into it. Don't be discouraged and don't give up. Keep giving and sending it. If anything comes to mind, take a few minutes to reflect upon it and then breathe it out before you get back to sending and receiving love.

Once you master giving and receiving love from people you already like or feel close to, start sending love to people you don't really like or care for. When you do this, you will raise your vibration from one of anger, fear or pain to one of love. You can also send and receive love from all humanity, and the world.

This exercise can also be done, when you enter into a room. Breathe in as you tell yourself "everyone in this room loves me" and breathe out with the words "and I love everyone in this room". It's amazing how this can make you feel and how your attitude changes. You will notice the effect by the way people in this room approach and respond to you.

3.5 Overcome ideas that hold you captive where you are.

To overcome any idea that holds you captive in any way possible you must first understand what is meant with "idea", and know and accept that this idea is present.

Throughout history the concept of idea is discussed and analyzed. It is said that the capacity to create and understand the meaning of ideas is considered to be an essential and defining feature of human beings.

In simple terms an idea arises in a reflex. In a spontaneous manner, it arises, even without thinking or serious reflection. This happens, for instance; when we talk about the idea of a person or a place.

In a more philosophical but still somewhat down to earth manner, John Locke, in his masterpiece *"An Essay Concerning Human Understanding"* defines idea as *'That term which, I think, serves best to stand for whatsoever is the object of the understanding when a man thinks, I have used it to express whatever is meant by phantasm, notion, species, or whatever it is which the mind can be employed about in thinking; and I could not avoid frequently using it.'*

Plato considered the concept of idea in the realm of metaphysics and its implications for epistemology. He claimed that there is a realm of forms or Ideas, which exists independently of anyone who may have thought of these ideas. Material things are then imperfect and transient reflections or instantiations of the perfect and unchanging ideas. From this it follows that these Ideas are the principal reality. In contrast to the individual objects of sense experience, which undergo constant change and flux, Plato held that ideas are perfect, eternal, and immutable. Consequently, Plato considered that knowledge of material things is not really knowledge; real knowledge can only be had of unchanging ideas.

Here we have two different views, spread accross two thousand five hundred years. And still we are struggling with the concept of idea. For the purpose of the CARE system I choose to assert that idea is one of the many whispers of consciousness that we in a moment of clarity spontaneously hear. It gives us a quick glimpse at the most obvious direction to choose by way of a candle light in the distance already fading. This is why quick action is necessary. But by the time we hesitate and try to analyze the viability of this idea the candle burns out, leaving us once again in the dark. Then through our thoughts we try to give meaning to the idea. However, the meaning we give is influenced by our past. We dissect the idea and reduce the separated parts to simple thoughts. Eventually they become one of the many constant thoughts we carry around until they eventually become our reality.

You see, ideas themselves do not hold us captive; they are like the stars in the sky shining pure light to give us direction in the dark. However, the meaning we choose to give to these ideas is what holds us captive. These meanings we produce come from our thoughts which in combination with our experiences and emotions become our truth. But then a funny thing happens; in our attempt to keep the meaning alive we start to build structures of thoughts that once in a while show themselves as a knight in shining armor. And as we are confused we mistakenly call these knights our ideas. This is how an idea, becomes a collection of thoughts, which arises in a spontaneous manner. And it is these thoughts that must be overcome if we want to move on from where we are to where we want to be.

3.6 Revisit the creative process.

I hope it is now clear to you how we delude ourselves every step of the way. We, in desperation, hold on to the idea that the light that once shined in the dark for us, to guide us to our present successes is the only light that will ever shine. Out of fear that this light will soon burn-out we fight hard to keep it alive and continue to follow this light of the past. However, as this light is one of the past we, without knowing, turn our backs to the future while we search for direction. This is how we become blind to the light and deaf to the whispers that guide us to the way that lies ahead of us.

I know; this is what makes it so confusing. Because, while you look to the past, the past is ahead of you which makes it logical to assume that you are searching in the right direction for the light.

However, when I say the light and whisper ahead of you I mean the light at the end of the road you must travel to get where you want to be, and the constant and silent whispers echoing along this road.

You might also be confused when I say; revisit the creative process. It is possible for you to think I mean go back in time and restart the process of creating.

But what I really mean is that once you accept the present moment to be your starting point and accept the fact that the idea that you have created is one based on the knight in shining armor; understand that this is OK, acknowledge this and be thankful for having that experience.

Once you accept and embrace these facts you will automatically open yourself to listen to what is being whispered, see what is being shown, feel whatever love is being vibrated and once more without effort start the process of creating.

This time you will know that what you are to create is what IDEA truly is. Because now you are conscious of how to use your Imagination to hear the whispers of consciousness, decide to do what is needed to follow the light ahead of you at the end of the road, expect nothing and receive the joy that comes with this experience.

You will not waste time putting care into analyzing the process. Instead you will LIVE the process and accept the results of your creation with open arms.

3.7 Enhance your idea.

At the beginning of Bridge to success I discussed the power of knowledge and the power of Imagination. I even went as far as suggesting that Albert Einstein's formula $E=MC^2$ and his explanation of this formula can be used in relation to imagination and knowledge. In my view they are also both but different manifestations of the same thing.

By linking imagination to the intention of consciousness I showed you the origin of imagination. What I didn't do was show you also the origin of knowledge.

This slipped my mind and so I made a mistake. Why I am mentioning this here is for two reasons.

1. Plato, by saying that knowledge of material things is not really knowledge; real knowledge can only be had of unchanging ideas, gave me an idea about how to explain this in a simple way.

   What Plato is actually saying is that pure knowledge like Idea comes direct from consciousness or GOD, which ever you prefer. Add to this that through the process of imagination we open the window between the physical and the spiritual world. And by doing so we hope to hear the whisper, see the images and feel the love. This process can simply be captured in one word; CREATION.

The whisper that comes from consciousness contains his knowledge and through his consistent whisper he shares this knowledge with you. The Images are the images of consciousness's intentions with and for us. To show us the ease by which we too can create with no effort.

The love is the expression of what consciousness experiences while engaged in the process of creation. This love is vibrated in a constant and everlasting manner for all that lives to experience. And once you combine the power of these three gifts you receive every day, directly from CONSCIOUSNESS, you will have enhanced your IDEA to its fullest.

2. The second reason is to show that making mistakes is an important part of the process. Life is a process of having an experience, not for the purpose of holding on to life. But for the purpose of going from being limited back to being limitless or

being time bound and traveling back to being timeless.

As long as we are alive it is our duty to LIVE which is part two (APPLY) of the CARE System. LIVE your IDEA and allow yourself to experience the mistakes along the way. Because only through these mistakes you will find joy when you take the next step and start to REFLECT.

This is how you bring to life the active part of CARE; **C**reate **A**pply and **R**eflect. Now all you need is the **E**nergy to fuel this car. Then you can drive it effortlessly into the realm of pure potentiality.

4 Energy

Consciousness is an activity of the entire universe, which means that when you are aware of everything, the universe is aware through you.

-Deepak Chopra-

4.1 Behave according to your core values.

Conscious or unconscious, overt or covert, voluntary or involuntary, every day we act or react to our environment. We tend to use social norms, which in fact are the collective writings on our walls, to evaluate the acceptability of our behavior, as these actions and reactions are called. We even try to regulate it by means of social control. However, our behavior, in sociology, is considered to be the most basic human action. And therefore our belief systems exert a greater control on our behavior than specific laws or social structures.

4.1.1 Belief, the driving force behind behavior

Through our behavior we express who we are, at least who we believe ourselves to be. This is where our belief system is externalized, ready to be judged by the outside world. This is where the expression of your belief becomes your behavior. This process starts when belief triggers your emotions and determines your behavior or actions.

You see, the feeding ground for our behavior lies in the intentions that transcend the barrier of time. But because of limitations we fabricate and accept, during the course of our lives, we create our reality based not on the original intentions of consciousness but on our limited interpretation of these intentions. We do this through our constant thoughts which are aimed at finding meaning and categorizing our interpretations with the sole purpose of creating our truth or belief system.

The driving force behind all of our behaviors is our belief. This is why our belief plays such an important role in our lives.

Unfortunately 96% of what we believe, we do without even understanding why. Therefore it follows that we are but 4% aware of our behavior and the effect thereof, not only on ourselves but on our environment. A logical conclusion is that almost 100% of our behavior is based on unconscious belief.

The challenge we now face is to be conscious of the true message hidden in our intentions. Program your reticular formation, also known as antennae, to tune in to every possible frequency. Eliminate all possible distortions by detaching the negative emotions that keep the thoughts alive of all the ways in which others cheated you, fought against you, degraded you or angered you. For as long as you allow these thoughts to be present in your life, your heart will forever be filled with hatred. Learn to let go and be happy, only then will you be better able to understand what you are truly intended to be.

To do this you must, besides understand the process through which your belief system was created, know that there are four different types of beliefs and understand the complexity of these systems. They are all intertwined with eachother in such a way that makes it difficult to notice each separately.

There are the Identity beliefs, Specific beliefs, Rules beliefs and Global beliefs. These four types of belief are like Siamese twins not only fighting for their own survival but at the same time for the survival of the others, even when the beliefs are conflicting.

Identity Beliefs

> The belief that has the largest impact on your behavior is the belief you have about who you are. This belief is very

powerful and the most challenging one to treat. However, once you understand how to change this belief about yourself you will have addressed many other issues that are linked with the other three. In fact the other three beliefs eventually act in support of the identity beliefs.

Specific Beliefs

Specific beliefs are beliefs you have about a certain person, object or happening. This belief is directly related to something specific and therefore the influence that it has can be limited toward this person, object or happening.

Global Beliefs

These beliefs are commonly used in generalizations. It is the belief you have about a certain group, like all women are…, all men are…, all blonds are…, all children are…, etc.

Rules Beliefs

In life we very often accept roles like father, mother, wife, husband, teacher etc. For each of these roles there are rules by which we must play, if we expect to be successful at this role. What we believe these rules to be, determines how we act them out.

You've come a long way and so far, I believe you understand the power of Imagination and Knowledge and the importance of uniting these two elements in the process of being one with yourself. You know that you are who you are intended to be, but misinterpretations delude you into following your shadow instead of the path of intention, that will get you there effortlessly. You have decided to search for the light in front of you, instead of the one that casts your shadow at your feet making it difficult for you not to follow your shadow. You should now understand that before you achieve your goals you must first set them. And to do this you must first face the challenge to escape from the doubts and fears that holds you captive in your limiting beliefs.

Now that you are able to set goals you must clarify your own values, understand and express what is the most important to you in your life. Only then can your goals truly be yours and every sub goal you set will fit perfectly, bringing you step by step closer to that ultimate goal. Once your goals are set you can plan how to get there, but make sure to commit yourself to your goals.

There is, however, one thing you must be aware of and that is not to replace the joy of the journey towards your ultimate goal with an obsession to rigidly follow the plan. The plan is not the objective; it is merely a tool that will help you get to where you want to be. However, even though sticking to the plan is not the objective, the experience of taking the drive on the highway of life is just as important as reaching the goal. Therefore it is most important that you enjoy the drive.

Now you are ready to take action and express yourself.

4.2 Express your true identity

The process of writing *Bridge to Success* for me has been and still is an inspiration in which, in my attempt to understand the true meaning of CARE, I have taken it totally apart and analyzed every component I could find. To show you what I mean I've made an overview of all the elements which together form the basis of the CARE system. Take a look at the following figure and you will see the CARE System structure;

Fig. 4.			
Create (Create your Idea)	**A**pply (Live your Idea)	**R**eflect (Explore your Idea)	**E**nergy (Be genuinely you)
Imagination	Learn	Effect	Behavior
Decision	Initiative	X-Factor	Expression
Expectation	Verify	People	Intention
Analysis	Energy	Love	Negotiate
		Overcome	Genuine
		Revisit	
		Enhance	

You might have noticed that this book is structured in the same way the CARE system is presented in this overview. And you also may have noticed that each component is interactive and is not restricted to the column it was assigned to.

While analyzing and putting this process on paper I experienced the same sense of timelessness as I did when I was a child. I also experienced the same uncontrollable urge to understand what made my treasured prize TIMEX watch tick, or where do the images come from on the TV screen, or whatever other reasons I then used to allow me to dismantle and reassemble the many objects I've tackled in the course of my childhood, during my quest for knowledge.

To me that was how I then expressed my true identity and as a child I never cared for the thought of not expressing this pureness. I heard the whispers, saw the images and felt the feelings clearly and so I expressed them. No time was reserved for conflict, it was a time for doing, being and expressing all that I knew, imagined and felt. There was never a doubt in my mind that what I've heard, seen or felt was not intended for me to express.

It wasn't until that day in the ditch that I started hiding my true identity in an attempt to survive the unknown. Now I know; to be in the unknown is exactly where you must be when you really want to live. Because living is learning and learning means to become aware of the unknown.

The logical conclusion is; to become aware of the unknown you must in fact put care and attention into the unknown. To be afraid of the unknown, as most of us are, means to be afraid to live your life and express who you really are.

The way I dealt with this fear for many years was to build walls around me and I allowed no one in. Like me, there are billions of people who use different tricks to cover up this fear. This is how we program ourselves to express who we are in ways we believe others expect us to, instead of who we really are. The result is that we allow our fears for the unknown to push us away from the highway of intention into hiding our true identity.

Imagine yourself to be one of these people. During your childhood, for the first time, in response to a discomforting situation, you choose to respond different with the unconscious intention of hiding your true identity for fear of the unknown.

This substitute response brings you comfort and slowly but surely you start to use this type of response often and it continues to bring comfort. Is it logical to conclude that this new response eventually becomes your preferred response?

I believe this is what happens. And beside the influence it has on your behavior, reactions and your lifestyle, it can also, in order to fill the gap between your true self and how you express yourself to be, cause you to become an excessive drinker, use drugs, gamble, lie, compulsive behavior or even cause physical or mental ailments.

This is why it is important to be aware of any turning point in your life where you cross the bridge of innocence into the world of the unknown.

This doesn't mean you should not cross that bridge. It means you must be aware when in this process and make sure that your reaction doesn't automatically lead you away from your true self.

Notice the discomfort, and even though you're new reaction brings comfort, realize, a reaction is what it is, and reactions do not add to the creative process. No CARE or attention is put into reactions. And notice that the trigger for this new action was discomfort. So, do not allow the comfort that it brought you in this specific situation become your new beacon in the dark.

Remember earlier I explained about how to use the energy that you create as your compass?

But before you do, make sure this energy is created with CARE and focused on the positive development of your true self. That self your consciousness intended you to be.

4.3 Make your intentions clear on every level.

Now I want to take a step back to find out who the driver is of the car ready to race full speed ahead over life's highway.

This simple question "Who am I, or in your case, who are you?" might seem trivial. But do you realize that this one question passed through the minds of 100% of every human being at one time or another during the course of our lives?

In the first chapter I showed you how to create possibilities and set goals for yourself. Now take a moment and look at these goals; notice that each and every one of them owes their existence to one single component which is; intention.

In the cycle of life the reason for knowing who you are is to learn how to work together with yourself and others. And as intention is not only at the root of all creative processes but also at the root of all knowledge gathering and maintaining processes I can safely conclude that your intentions contains at least 95% of the DNA that can tell us who you really are. In the search for your identity, would it then not be safe to take a closer look at your intentions?

What they are, how they come about and where they put you in the grand scheme of things.

4.3.1 Circumstances.

Let us recap; Intention is the pavement over which imagination and knowledge travel. When imagination and knowledge join forces and exist in harmony with each other, they become the vehicle (CAR) fueled with belief, or in the first stage, presumed intention: that part of intention that lives within the physical world.

You see the highway of intention is always present for each and everyone to travel across. However, for some this path is more visible than for others. The light that shines on the pavement of intention is expectation. Which not only brings us light in the dark but also acts as a compass telling us where is north, south, east or west.

Let's now take a look at Prince Charles of The United Kingdom. When he was born what did the world expect of him? Did he have a choice to expect anything else? What does the world expect of him to become today? What is the difference between the first expectation and the latter? Why did the world expect Prince Charles to become King?

The circumstances we find ourselves in are important building blocks with which we build our expectations;

On December 10th, 2003 Queen Beatrix of the Netherlands was blessed with the birth of her first grandchild. By Dutch law, Princess Amalia became second to the throne after her father, Prince Willem Alexander. Based on this fact, the public and the world expect her to become the next queen of the Netherlands, after Queen Beatrix and her father's subsequent reigns, as Queen and King. As time goes by, circumstances change, and also expectations, as we can see with Prince Charles.

At this point in time, it is a process that takes place only in our minds; the fact that Princess Amalia (should she even understand the situation) and the world, expect her to become Queen of the Netherlands. Before this expectation can become a reality some actions need to be taken to ensure the circumstances continue to allow everyone to remain having this expectation.

Amalia's belief system must be programmed in such a way that there is no doubt in her mind that she is intended to be the next queen of the Netherlands. To fulfill this intention, she must learn what it means to be queen, understand the responsibilities that lay on her shoulders, take these responsibilities serious, live, think, walk and talk like a queen. While her parents, Willem Alexander and Maxima maintain and if needed recreate new circumstances that will have us continue to expect Amalia to be our Queen. Also her parents must guide her through her doubts and help her to remove all obstacles along the way. As you can see, building the bridge between expectation and reality becomes a joint effort.

Take a close look at the situation with Princess Amalia and you will see that her pavement of intention was instantly lit up by expectation, from the moment she was born. Our collective minds expect nothing else than the fact that Princess Amalia will become Queen of The Netherlands. Once this expectation reached the mind of a critical mass (I will explain what this means later), the energy generated from this thought reflects back onto this little girl, whose highway of intention instantly becomes visible, not only to her, but to everyone else.

4.3.2 Critical mass.

Ken Keyes, Jr. wrote in his book "The Hundredth Monkey" about scientists who had been observing monkeys in the wild for thirty years. In 1952, on the island of Koshima, when there was a serious drought & famine, the scientists provided monkeys with sweet potatoes which they dropped in the sand. The monkeys liked the taste of the potatoes but found the sand unpleasant. One day, an eighteen month old monkey washed the potatoes in a nearby stream. She taught the trick to her mother and her playmates, who taught it to their mothers. As the story is told, it lasted about six years, between 1952 and 1958, before 99 monkeys learned to wash their sweet potato. Until one day the 100th monkey learned the trick. Suddenly, almost every monkey on the island began to wash their potatoes before eating them. The added energy of this 100th monkey had somehow created a behavioral breakthrough. But, it was more amazing for the scientists to observe that colonies of monkeys on other islands as far as 500 miles away, began washing their sweet potatoes, while there was no way for these monkeys to have contact with monkeys on other islands.

This phenomenon is known as "critical mass." When a limited number of people know something in a new way, it remains the conscious property of only those people. However, there is a point at which if only one more person tunes in to a new awareness, that new awareness is picked up by everyone without going through the standard learning process.

Sometimes, even though this new awareness is available for everyone to pick up, some cannot find the right frequency that would enable them to receive this awareness. Or in many cases the interpretation of this information is misformed in such a way that it cannot be applied effectively. It is as if the light that is shined on the pavement of our intentions (intended to show us the direction to take) is deflected by what we expect. We must realize that expectation is like a compass invented to steer us away from danger. But the magnets in the compass of expectation respond the strongest to circumstances you find yourself in, your mind set and behavior from your parents.

Understand; when each of these three elements produce a different expectation there will be conflict and you will be stuck. Take a look at how the situation with Prince Charles evolved during his lifetime and you will notice a perfect illustration of this point.

4.3.3 Who are you and your intentions?

The seven qualities to posses, to master the art of intention, that Deepak Chopra talked about in his book "How to know God" contains valuable life lessons.

For your convenience I will repeat them here;

1. They do not attach to the past or possible outcome of a situation.

2. They adapt rapidly to mistakes or bad judgments.

3. They have highly sensitive antennea and notice even the smallest signs.

4. There is a good connection between their spirit and body.

5. They do not have any problems with the acceptance of uncertainty or ambiguity.

6. They patiently await the results of their wishes while fully confident in the universe.

7. They make karmic connections and are able to understand the meaning of coincidental occurrences.

Look in the mirror and ask yourself what do I see? Do I see someone who has mastered the art of intention? How many of these seven qualities do you possess? Or is the struggle to find the hidden gems within ongoing?

Do you believe you can know yourself without understanding the nature of your intentions?

And even if you understand the nature of your intentions, can you know who you are? You may have noticed that finding out who you are in this physical setting raises more questions than it brings answers.

I believe that, to find who you really are you must let go of the restricting idea you have about who your physical self is and allow the possibility that you are much more than you can imagine.

The seven steps mentioned by Deepak Chopra bring you a long way toward finding yourself. However, it is my belief that intention lives partly in the physical world and partly in the spiritual world. And this is what makes it so difficult for us to understand who we are. When we interpret the meaning of our intentions, we do so while our minds are tuned into a frequency of the physical world. As long as we do not use the power of imagination by way of visualization, meditation or any other means, which is in fact; to tune in on a spiritual frequency, we will miss much of the information sent to us on spiritual frequencies and the part we do pick up will be misinterpreted.

In my view, intention lives partially in the above mentioned worlds simultaneously which forms the gateway to and from the spiritual world.

During one of his seminars, Stanford University Professor Dr. William A. Tiller, spoke about his views concerning spiritual and physical self.

He explained; *"we are all spirits having a physical experience together, as we ride the river of life. Our spiritual parents dressed us in our bio body suites and put us in this play pin which we call a universe, in order to grow in coherence, develop our gifts of intentionality and to become what we are intended to become, that is co creators with our spiritual parents. These bio body suits come in a variety of colors and two general unique forms which we call genders and they have four layers. There is the outer electric monopole layer (substance layer). The first inner layer is the magnetic monopole substance layer. The second inner layer is the emotion substance layer and the third inner layer is the mind substance layer, and inside of that is a portion of our spirit self which in essence drives the vehicle."*

What I understand from this is that who I really am lies in the intention of a spiritual entity. Part of this spiritual entity is shielded from the rest by the four layers that are not coherent, which causes the communication flow between this separated part and the rest of the spiritual entity to be disrupted. To restore the communication it is the job of my spirit self, which is separated from the rest, to restore coherence between the four layers, my spirit self and the rest of the spirit entity I am part of.

Dr. Tiller's conclusion after more than 30 years of scientific research offers the tool to substantiate what I've said about where intention lives. It is a scientific approach to spirituality that I find very interesting.

Also Albert Einstein's view on this matter was expressed in the following way;

"A human being is part of a whole, called by us the Universe, a part limited in time and space. He experiences himself, his thoughts and feelings, as something separated from the rest; a kind of optical delusion of his consciousness. This delusion is a kind of prison for us, restricting us to our personal desires and to affection for a few persons nearest us. Our task must be to free ourselves from this prison by widening our circles of compassion to embrace all living creatures and the whole of nature in its beauty."

Even though the wording is slightly different the meaning is about the same. I can carry on forever on this subject but as it is my intention to write a practical guide to success, and not a book about spirituality or science I will not go into further details about this.

For now see yourself as a diamond in the rough with one spark of light at its core, doing what comes natural, continually shining, reaching out to connect with any light that comes from the outside. Once this spark of light reconnects with the source from which it originated, there will be nothing else but light.

4.3.4 Who is driving your car?

Remember in the introduction I warned that the information in this book will get you but 80% on the way to your personal success and 20% is your responsibility? Well this is why; every once in a while people ask me if it doesn't get to me; the negative vibes that goes with conflict and the fact that I am so often involved with people who during their conflict, want to attack each other? In my experience as a mediator, I've come to understand that it is just the opposite. My clients do not want to attack each other; they actually want to find a solution for the situation that divides them. And they are to some extent conscious of their intentions. However, in their communication they lack the ability to express these intentions in a manner that will allow for, not only theirs, but also the other party's intentions to grow from intention through imagination and/or knowledge to belief and finally crystallize into their common goals.

To explain what I mean I will now ask you to see yourself as the driver of your car on the highway of life. Along the way you make stops to enjoy the scenery and meet others. Every once in a while you pick up a passenger, with whom you drive part of the way and enjoy the trip leading to your final destiny. Now picture for a moment that you picked up a passenger with whom during the drive the relationship evolves. And you decide to go all the way with this person.

At a certain moment while you approach a roundabout, you switch on your signal light to go right. When the signal goes on you notice your passenger gazing at the light as it goes tic, tack, tic, tack, and (s)he starts behaving nervous as you come closer and closer to the roundabout. One second before you turn the steering wheel to go to the right your passenger, in a panic calls out; go straight ahead! This sudden request and the intensity with which it was delivered confuses you.

But being the good host you are, you decide to make a full circle at the roundabout to discuss the new situation, before you decide which way to go. One circle doesn't seem to give enough time to find a solution, so you go yet another hoping to get clarity to the situation. Now after your tenth time around the circle and getting nowhere in your communications with your passenger, you are irritated. And in your edginess you stop the car and ask him/her to get out of the car. To your surprise you are not the only person who is irritated and instead of stepping out of the car this person shouts back at you requesting you to get out of the car.

The dynamics in the communication shift swiftly from irritation to anger and within no time there seems to be a situation of pure hostility. With steam coming from your noses, the both of you urge the other to get out of the car. This is my car and I want you out of it. None of you mean to hurt the other but instead each of you intend to leave the hostile situation behind you and get on with your lives (car).

Notice how long it took to find out that you're going nowhere and, at the same time, how after only ten circles the focus quickly shifted from the question, what direction to choose to whose car it is.

Anyway, now take yourselves out of the car and picture a young family with two children in the same situation where one parent wants to go right and the other straight ahead. As you turn the steering wheel for the tenth time, ask yourself; is this your family or your wife/husbands? Who is the passenger and who the owner of the car (substitute car with this life)? Whose life is being lived and who is living it? These are all questions asking us to take a closer look at the relationships we are in. But more important, they ask us to look at the responsibility we have in making sure that all of our intentions are clear to all of our co-passengers, and to accept this responsibility. One way to take responsibility is to put full attention and Care in your communication, not only with others, but also with yourself.

4.4 Go for win-win through negotiations.

Often when we think about negotiations, our minds take us to business or organizational negotiations, legal proceedings and negotiations among nations. Less frequently negotiations have been recognized in personal situations such as marriage, divorce, parenting, and everyday life. However, with the growth of alternative dispute resolution, of which mediation is a part, negotiation is becoming more accepted in personal situations.

Now let us take a look at the definitions of negotiation according to;

The Oxford English Dictionary;

Try to reach an agreement or compromise by discussion.

Wikipedia;

Negotiation is a dialogue intended to resolve disputes, to produce an agreement upon courses of action, to bargain for individual or collective advantage, or to craft outcomes to satisfy various interest.

Discussion and dialogue are active parts of these two definitions and both are restricted manners of communicating. When putting it in a broader perspective, this in fact brings us to the following definition; negotiation is to communicate with a specific purpose of reaching an agreement.

To take it one step further I will take the liberty to add; the purpose of this agreement is to instigate specific behavior or action.

Now take a moment to go back to part one of Bridge to Success where you learned to create your IDEA. Do you realize that during this process of creation, eighty percent of your energy went into internal dialogue or communication with yourself?

Before, during and after every action you take, you will communicate with yourself. Every thought you have is a communication process. Whenever a connection is made between an event and an emotion, which in turn triggers an action, this is a communication process.

But all of these and so many other unconscious internal communication processes, we choose to neglect. In fact, internal communication is just as important, if not more important, to be conscious of than all communications we have with others.

Simply put, communication is a process of transferring information from one entity to another.

4.4.1 Obstacles in communication

Because the word communication is often misunderstood and frequently used inappropriately, I will be clear about what I mean with communication. For me communication is a continuous process of working together, by use of emotions, thoughts, experience, and words, towards a mutually accepted goal.

Before you can have effective communication there are four obstacles that need to be addressed; 1. I already know. 2. The absence of mass. 3. The level is too high and 4. Word misunderstood.

a) I already know.

- This looks familiar doesn't it? It should in any case. In chapter one I discussed the power of knowledge and how the interaction between knowledge and imagination can disrupt the internal communication. Even though "I already know" doesn't necessarily mean I know based on scientific facts. Just the mere idea that I think I know what to expect will disrupt the communication. You see, when I think I know what to expect, I will automatically, through my actions, reject the information that is being shared with me. Imagine yourself enthusiastically telling your friend a story about this new course you've followed, the effect it had on you and what you have decided to do as a result of this course. And this person is the first person you choose to share this important information with. Unless your friend is a psychic and can read your mind (s)he cannot know the content or the information you want to share. So how does it make you feel when your friend doesn't seem to make any effort to understand what you are talking about? Do you still want to share your experience with him/her? To overcome this obstacle your friend must learn to let go. Because as long as (s)he continues to cling on to his/her idea of what the outcome of a situation will be, all other possibilities are being stifled. This illustrates the effect one has on others when one does not master the art of intention fully. Remember; people who have mastered the art of intention do not attach to the past or possible outcome of a situation.

b) The absence of mass.

- Do you recognize the situation where you are at a party where you're introduced to a lot of new people, colleagues, their partners and friends of your spouse? During the course of the evening, while listening to yet another story, you start getting tired and feel your body just start to hang like dead weight. You see the person in front of you talking but feel bored and catch yourself just staring ahead seeing the lips move but the words can't find their way to your ears? This kind of boredom is caused by the lack of mass, which means there is nothing in the information received that you can identify with. What do you do when you are in this kind of situation? The most of us shut down all brain activity, go into automatic pilot and show our polite side; once in a while we nod or say aha, while we look for the right moment to get away. But what does this do for the communication? I'm sure the communication was dead from the moment you could not identify with the information. How can you bring life into the communication? Actually this is easy. You add mass by making the information tangible. Ask the speaker to give examples and if you still cannot identify, get a pencil and paper and start to draw what you think (s)he means and ask for confirmation. You can even ask him/her to draw his/her thoughts. Could you imagine the change in dynamics as a result of this approach? Once you show the speaker that you are interested to understand what (s)he is talking about you make him/her conscious of his/her responsibility for the information he/she wants to share. So if (s)he feels the information so far was rubbish, (s)he will think twice before talking more about that. Instead (s)he will automatically try to understand what you want to know and make an effort to find the right way to communicate this to you.

c) The level is too high.

- Have you ever had the pleasure of being introduced to a scientific genius or a professional who for 80% of the time talks in the dialect only known to other scientific geniuses or other professionals in the same field? A simple example is the brain surgeon who explains to his patient, who is an accountant, what his diagnosis is in the following manner:

    "My diagnosis is that you suffer from Agenesis of Corpus Callosum. This means that a coronal section of the brain through the level of the midbrain showing agenesis or lack of development of the corpus callosum during intrauterine life".

    Do you feel yourself getting dizzy?

    Too often communication suffers under these conditions. This doesn't make the accountant less intelligent than the brain surgeon It just means that both of them need to tune into a different frequency than that of their respective professions. They need to work together towards the mutually accepted goal of getting the correct message across and understanding what the message is. To do this, it is the accountant's responsibility to ask the brain surgeon to go back to the last point from where he couldn't understand. The surgeon's responsibility is to find out if the accountant understands what has been said and if not, go back to the point from where the accountant couldn't understand. Also the surgeon must continue to reformulate the information until the message is clear and fully understood. He also must confirm with the accountant that the information is fully understood.

d) Word misunderstood.

- In a previous chapter I talked about knowledge holding you hostage. Now I will show you how imagination can also do the same. Think about a conversation you recently had with someone and as the conversation goes on, you find yourself wondering; what does that word mean? So, in your mind you search for the meaning by looking through your dictionary or picturing situations where you might have heard or read this word before. What mostly happens in these kind of situations, is that we are so focused on finding the meaning of that word; we use 95% of our attention thinking about it. At the same time we refuse to allow the other person to know that we do not know the meaning of this word and end up driving continually in circles at the roundabout going nowhere (EGO). All information that was passed on to us from the moment this misunderstood word captured our attention is lost. You find yourself yawning, irritated, having headaches, stomach aches, restless, the muscles in your face collaps and you want to leave. What does this all do for the communication? I'm sure you will agree that there is no communication without attention. This is a very simple example of how communication loses it's effectiveness, when in fact these types of situations can be solved in a simple way. Whenever you find yourself distracted by a word you do not understand, during a conversation, just ask the person who used the word to explain what his/her definition of that word is.

4.4.2 Effective use of communication

The above mentioned four obstacles have an effect on all of the communication channels; emotions, thoughts, experience, and words. This makes it important to understand that effective communication calls for you to;

I. Be present and conscious of the moment of now. Put all of your attention in that moment. In fact 80% of all communication is attention.

II. Be analytical, observe and see or hear what you've seen or heard and not what you think you've seen or heard. To explain what I mean please imagine that we are in the middle of the forest in the winter. It is freezing cold and we are well dressed to protect us from the cold. I am standing in front of you. With my right arm stretched to the side of my body in a horizontal position. And I ask you to look at my outstretched arm and tell me what you see, the most common answer will be a generalization based on assumptions such as; I see your right arm. Some will add to that; and at the end of your arm I see your hand with fingers. Even though this might sound like the correct answer, it is not. Because in fact, yes, my arm is stretched out, but it is covered by the arm sleeve of my thick winter jacket and my hand and fingers are kept warm by the gloves I use to keep my fingers from freezing off. So what do you see when you look at my arm?

III. Accept the things as they are. If you do not understand something ask for clarification. Do not enslave the facts to your belief system. Allow the interaction to evolve in a natural way towards finding the road to a win-win outcome.

IV. Communicate with the intention of being understood. Avoid all attempts to suppress, belittle or deprive someone of their right. Imagine someone trying to suppress, belittle or deprive you the chance of being right. I'm sure this experience will make you feel under attack. Now as we know, survival is one of the clearest instructions everything that lives understands. Wouldn't it be safe to conclude that any kind of threat to your existence will consciously or unconsciously be eliminated in an attempt to survive? This could only result in mutual attempts to eliminate each other instead of effective communication.

V. Duplicate your process and show understanding for the counterparts by making it a point to allow issues and people to be important. One way to do this is by asking for help. It is in the nature of humans to help. Situations like immediately after the Tsunami of Christmas 2004, where a few hundred thousand people died and millions were left homeless and other major disasters around the globe, where the reaction of the world is to gather as much possible funds, people and material to help the victims, show that whenever there is a crisis situation, people's natural reaction is to offer help. However, in our day to day lives we are so focused on taking care of our safety, we don't pay much attention to where help is needed and we do not expect help to be given to us. But what we should realize is, that by asking for help, you acknowledge the person you ask to help you in his/her existence and by doing so, increase his/her chances to survive. And ultimately you give this person the opportunity to CARE.

VI. Always confirm that there is a mutual understanding and make sure that any room for misunderstanding is taken away. By doing so, you personally take responsibility for your role and make the other party conscious of his/her responsibility.

By addressing each of these elements during all of your communications, you ensure yourself of doing everything that is needed to make your communication successful.

But remember your task is to create coherence between all levels of your existence. By doing so you restore the connection between your essence and the source from which you were created.

Beside the above mentioned elements of communication, there is one important element, which was discussed extensively in a previous chapter: Imagination.

Practice meditation, chi gong, yoga or visualization in preparation of all communication processes and you will achieve the silence needed to find the true meaning of your intentions. And as communication is aimed at understanding and making intentions clear, you should look within yourself for the true meaning of your intentions. Only then can you effectively, through communication, open the channels for others to tap into the source of your goals, enabling them to work together with you to find the way to get you there.

4.5 Be genuinely you.

Take a look at the picture below as I explain. This drawing is the cross section of a tree. You can see a timeline represented by the year rings which tells us the age of the tree. Every year that passes by, a new ring develops pushing the bark and the outer bark further away from the heart. When you take a walk in the forest, looking at the trees, all you see is the outer bark, branches, leaves and fruits. And you consider this to be the tree.

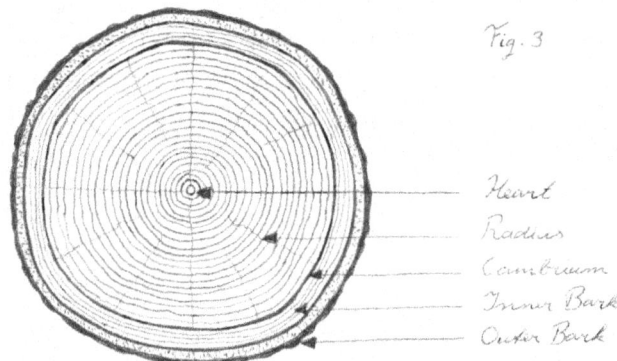

Fig. 3
Heart
Radius
Cambium
Inner Bark
Outer Bark

But ask yourself while looking at this picture, which part is the purest part of the tree from this perspective. Is it the outer bark, the inner bark, cambium, radius or the heart of the tree? When you look at a tree, do you see the tree or the outer bark? Is the outer bark that you see the essence of the tree? If not, then how far back in time must you travel to see the part that is the essence of the tree?

Take a closer look at the process of this tree becoming a tree. Let us assume that each particle of this tree, no matter how small or large, put together represents the true essence or character of this tree.
This five hundred year old tree went through a process of becoming a five hundred year old tree, able to genuinely be the five hundred year old tree you now see before you.

When the tree was one hundred, fifty, ten, or five years old, then, in its totality was it not a tree of that age? Even when it was still under the ground finding its way to the surface of the earth, was it then not a genuine tree of that age?

Now take one more look at the picture above and ask yourself. What lies at the centre of the heart of this tree and consider that this is where this tree originated from.

Now that we have established that this five hundred year old tree was, is and always, in its totality, has been genuinely a tree with it's origin at the centre of its heart, take a moment to imagine.

Imagine that, what lies at the centre of the heart, through which this tree became a five hundred year old tree, is of the same matter that, every day, caresses the bark of the tree. Imagine that this tiny portion that lies at the core of the heart is the same towards which the tree reaches out; growing taller and broader every year a new ring appears.

And if this five hundred year old tree is genuinely a five hundred year old tree because of the sum of all its components, and all of its components represent everything and nothing at the same time, then to me the essence or character of this tree lies in the intention consciousness had with its projection of this tree.
In my limited wisdom I believe this tree has fulfilled its intentions perfectly. For five hundred years this tree expressed the potential

of becoming anything that we can imagine it to be; supplier of oxygen, source of energy, beauty in a landscape, shade, shelter, table, chair, supplier of food (the fruit it gives us), warmth in the winter (wood for the fireplace), the floor in our home, the walls of our home, a plate, decorations or whatever else you can imagine, this tree effortlessly will become.

4.5.1 What is at the centre of your heart?

The metaphor I used in the previous section illustrates how we humans also, as each year passes by, grow further away from the core from which we originated. This alarms us as we, contrary to the tree, do not realize that by physically expanding away from our heart centre in fact we are reaching out to reconnect with the same essence of ourselves that lies at the centre of our hearts.

In our search for truth we, instead, give all kinds of different meaning to this process and end up losing the conscious connection with what is at the centre of our hearts.

We simply forget that truth has different dimensions; beyond the limitations of time truth is nothing and everything. Within the limitations of time, truth is the manifestation of tomorrow as you imagine it to be; NOW!

By consciously losing connection, we step out of the realm of knowing, into the process of finding out, -having an experience or -living. This has been, and is, the choice of consciousness.

Like the tree, you are in fact composed of every single particle that you consist of, and like the tree you are also, at the same moment, everything and nothing.
Whatever you do, positive or negative, the end result will be the same; you are genuinely what you are. And as with the three, you must explore the potential you posses and become anything that you choose to imagine yourself to be.

All that is necessary is that you put CARE and attention into the process of your life. Then you will, in a conscious manner, enjoy the experience you set out to have. This is the experience of creation.

To be successful in this life you must in full consciousness have and become the experience. With the right CARE and attention you will become the success you were intended to be. It is the success of being genuine in who you are on all conceivable levels of your existence.

Experience yourself as the centre of the universe, free from hate, anger, fear, uncontrollable desires or any other limitations.

Care for, love and give as much attention that is needed to achieve whatever your heart desires. In the same way Care for others, love and give them the attention needed to achieve whatever their heart desires.

Only then will you effortlessly and consistently become much more than you can imagine being; you will then be genuinely a great Success!

5 Epilogue.

When you are who you are and everything you have in life is all that you need, then you are a success.

In *Bridge to Success*, I have taken you for a drive on life's highway, in my car. Along the way you were made conscious of the many roundabouts we so often end up stuck on; going around in circles.

I have also discussed how to determine your point of origin, your destination and how to build the bridge between where you are, now, in life and where you want to be. At the beginning of this book I mentioned that *Bridge to Success* will get you 80% of the way and 20% will be your responsibility.

I realize that even though you've read Bridge to Success the lessons learned will not, all at once, be retained and therefore putting them into practice will take some more CARE and Attention. Should you need help in this phase of the process then please do not hesitate to sign up for our newsletter via our website; http://www.jonesmc.nl/ or send an e-mail with questions you might have to help you gain affinity with the CARE system. Who knows maybe your questions will be the inspiration I need to write a CARE system's manual.

www.ingramcontent.com/pod-product-compliance
Lightning Source LLC
Chambersburg PA
CBHW070951180426
43194CB00042B/2249